SMALL GROUP SERIES

Lessons on Love

FOLLOWING CHRIST'S EXAMPLE

INTER*Actions*

SMALL GROUP SERIES

Lessons on Love

FOLLOWING CHRIST'S EXAMPLE

BILL HYBELS

WITH KEVIN & SHERRY HARNEY

WILLOW CREEK RESOURCES®

*Helping People Become
Fully Devoted to Christ*

ZondervanPublishingHouse
Grand Rapids, Michigan

A Division of HarperCollinsPublishers

Lessons on Love
Copyright © 1996 by the Willow Creek Association

Requests for information should be addressed to:

🏭 ZondervanPublishingHouse
Grand Rapids, Michigan 49530

ISBN: 0-310-20680-4

Zondervan Editors: Jack Kuhatschek and Rachel Boers
Willow Creek Editors: Bill Donahue and Mark Mittelberg
Interior design by Rick Devon

Printed in the United States of America

96 97 98 99 00 01 02 03/❖DC/10 9 8 7 6 5 4 3 2 1

CONTENTS

Interactions 7

Introduction: Following Christ's Example 9

SESSION 1
Loving Lessons 11

SESSION 2
Tender Love 19

SESSION 3
Tough Love 27

SESSION 4
Sacrificial Love 35

SESSION 5
Steadfast Love 43

SESSION 6
Radical Love 51

Leader's Notes 59

INTERACTIONS

In 1992, Willow Creek Community Church, in partnership with Zondervan Publishing House and the Willow Creek Association, released a curriculum for small groups entitled the Walking with God series. In just three years, almost a half million copies of these small group study guides were being used in churches around the world. The phenomenal response to this curriculum affirmed the need for relevant and biblical small group materials.

At the writing of this curriculum, there are over one thousand small groups meeting regularly within the structure of Willow Creek Community Church. We believe this number will increase as we continue to place a central value on small groups. Many other churches throughout the world are growing in their commitment to small group ministries as well, so the need for resources is increasing.

In response to this great need, the Interactions small group series has been developed. Willow Creek Association and Zondervan Publishing House have joined together to create a whole new approach to small group materials. These discussion guides are meant to challenge group members to a deeper level of sharing, create lines of accountability, move followers of Christ into action, and help group members become fully devoted followers of Christ.

SUGGESTIONS FOR INDIVIDUAL STUDY

1. Begin each session with prayer. Ask God to help you understand the passage and to apply it to your life.
2. A good modern translation, such as the New International Version, the New American Standard Bible, or the New Revised Standard Version will give you the most help. Questions in this guide are based on the New International Version.
3. Read and reread the passage(s). You must know what the passage says before you can understand what it means and how it applies to you.
4. Write your answers in the spaces provided in the study guide. This will help you to express clearly your understanding of the passage.
5. Keep a Bible dictionary handy. Use it to look up unfamiliar words, names, or places.

SUGGESTIONS FOR GROUP STUDY

1. Come to the session prepared. Careful preparation will greatly enrich your time in group discussion.
2. Be willing to join in the discussion. The leader of the group will not be lecturing, but will encourage people to discuss what they have learned in the passage. Plan to share what God has taught you in your individual study.
3. Stick to the passage being studied. Base your answers on the verses being discussed rather than on outside authorities such as commentaries or your favorite author or speaker.
4. Try to be sensitive to the other members of the group. Listen attentively when they speak, and be affirming whenever you can. This will encourage more hesitant members of the group to participate.
5. Be careful not to dominate the discussion. By all means participate! But allow others to have equal time.
6. If you are the discussion leader, you will find additional suggestions and helpful ideas in the leader's notes.

ADDITIONAL RESOURCES AND TEACHING MATERIALS

At the end of this study guide you will find a collection of resources and teaching materials to help you in your growth as a follower of Christ. You will also find resources that will help your church develop and build fully devoted followers of Christ.

INTRODUCTION: FOLLOWING CHRIST'S EXAMPLE

Most of us have taken lessons in a number of areas. You might have taken music lessons some time in your childhood. Maybe you learned to play an instrument or took vocal lessons. Maybe you have focused on some kind of recreational pursuit or hobby such as horseback riding, swimming, golf, skiing, cooking, dancing, or tennis. Maybe you took lessons that were a little less common: speed reading, painting, sculpting, acting, public speaking, polo, scuba diving, or karate. The fact is, you can take lessons to help you develop almost any skill imaginable.

One summer I got a little bored so I arranged to take a helicopter flying lesson. It was great fun. After forty-five minutes of scaring my instructor half to death, I got the hang of it... a little bit. At another point in my life I took Greek classes to help me understand the Bible better. I found it challenging and fun, too. These kinds of lessons keep us stimulated; they build our confidence; they add a little spice to life.

But if you think about it, most of the lessons we've taken aren't essential for leading a satisfied life. Most of us could get along just fine if we had to go without our golf lessons or dance lessons—activities that don't really make us or break us. What's ironic is that there seem to be so few classes offered in the substantial areas of life.

How many of us have taken lessons to help us become a better father, mother, parent, or friend? How many of us have taken a class designed to help us become a more loving person? Yet these are the areas that matter most.

I rarely have people come up to me after a church service with tears in their eyes and a broken heart because they're having trouble with their putting stroke. There are very few people who contemplate doing awful things because they can't master a certain dance step. But I do receive a steady stream of calls, visits, and letters from people who are in deep pain because they can't get along with a husband, wife, mother, dad, child, friend, boss, employee, in-law, neighbor, and even sometimes their pastor!

Why don't we have classes focused on loving better? Why don't we commit ourselves to a study that could really improve an area of life in which we are all involved? Why don't we focus on a topic that hits the core of our lives?

This series of interactions is designed to help you focus on one of the most important areas of life—loving relationships. If you are tired of shallow love and if you hunger for more loving relationships, this series of sessions is for you.

In these interactions you will learn the balance between tender love and tough love, both of which are essential for healthy relationships. You will also be invited to extend sacrificial love to others, the same kind of love Jesus has given you. You will also be challenged to develop a love for others that is steadfast and that will carry you through the tough times. Finally, you will meet a God who loves you with a radical love and who calls you to communicate this same love to others.

God's love is life-changing. Of all the lessons you could take at this time in your life, *Love: Following Christ's Example* may be the most important.

Bill Hybels

LOVING LESSONS

THE BIG PICTURE

When a building is being constructed, the groundwork is critically important. If the foundation is faulty, the whole building will be unstable. If the foundation is solid, the building will be stable and stand firm under stress.

The same is true when building loving relationships. We need to have a solid foundation on which to build. If we don't, the whole structure of the relationship is in danger. If we have a solid base of love, we can experience deep and meaningful relationships.

Although all of us desire to be genuinely loving, we all have different natural capacities for receiving and expressing love. If I were to teach a ski class, there would inevitably be a variety of skill levels displayed. Some people would barely be able to stand up. They would be falling over in the lift line, impaling themselves on their ski poles, or accidentally stabbing those around them. Others could negotiate the bunny slope with a certain amount of confidence. And then there would be those who could ski down the hills with ease and style. It doesn't bother us to think about how some people are better at a certain sport or activity. However, when it comes to loving, we assume everyone has acquired the same abilities and skills. The hard truth is that some people have a great natural ability to love, while others have to work at expressing love.

There are a variety of loving capacities among the members of your small group. This may be partly the result of how much love each received in their family as they were growing up. It is also determined by basic temperament and personality. Some of us have soft and gentle temperaments, while others do not.

Our capacity to love is also based on how we have responded to the things life has thrown at us. Life is a mixed bag. Some people encounter obstacles and difficulties and become increasingly bitter and hard-hearted over the years. Others tend to become more open and kind and gentle over time. In almost every group there will be those who are more naturally caring and kind and others who can be short-fused, calloused, and even a little tough-hearted. The majority of us are somewhere in the middle.

A WIDE ANGLE VIEW

1
Put an "X" on each line below to indicate where you would place the following people in relationship to their ability to feel and express love.

Your father

Tenderhearted   Tough-Hearted

├──┤

Expressive of love   Not expressive of love

├──┤

Your mother

Tenderhearted   Tough-Hearted

├──┤

Expressive of love   Not expressive of love

├──┤

You

Tenderhearted   Tough-Hearted

├──┤

Expressive of love   Not expressive of love

├──┤

Why did you choose to put the "X" where you did on each line?

LESSONS ON LOVE

A BIBLICAL PORTRAIT

Read Hebrews 10:22–25

2 In this passage we are called to "spur one another on toward love and good deeds." If you view your small group members as the "one another" in this passage, what can you do to "spur one another on" to be more loving?

SHARPENING THE FOCUS

Read Snapshot "You Matter to God!"

YOU MATTER TO GOD!

God wants to see each of us transformed into a more loving person. The first thing He does in this transformation process is convince you, to the core of your being, that you matter to Him. You are the focus of His affection. You are precious in His sight. You are loved beyond words.

When seekers turn to the Bible they find countless portions of Scripture where God takes a huge risk. He knows, with His omniscience, that certain people are going to reject His love, but He says it anyway. I like the way it is put in Isaiah 43, verses 1 and 4. God says through Isaiah, "I have summoned you by name ... You are precious and honored in my sight." And then there are the words "I love you." In a loveless world, God reaches out and says we matter more to Him than we could ever dream.

3 What would you say to a person in your small group to express to them how much they matter to God?

How do we show kids that they matter to God?

Read Snapshot "Love in Action"

LOVE IN ACTION

When it comes to love, God takes it far beyond just words. We all know that talk is cheap. God didn't demonstrate His love in some glittery, Hollywood style with soft colors and moving music in the background. God rolled up His sleeves, put on human flesh, and came to live among us. He became part of a family. He developed a trade as a carpenter. He became active in relationships. He came out of the heavenly grandstand and got knocked around on the playing field of life. This means that when we pray to Him, we can be assured that He knows all about family joys and struggles. He knows all about work. He knows all about relationships. We have rock-solid assurance that He understands. He truly has walked in our shoes.

Another reason God put on human flesh was to show people a purer kind of love than they had ever witnessed before. Love for the unlovely, the needy, the forgotten people, and love for sinners like you and me. Of course, in the supreme demonstration of love, He sacrificed Himself voluntarily and paid the penalty for our sins so that we could come into a relationship with the Father. "Greater love has no one than this, that he lay down his life for his friends" (John 15:13). If you miss this, you miss everything. When you become personally involved with this kind of love, when the scales fall off your eyes for the first time and this kind of love grips you and moves you and comes crashing into your soul, you will never be the same.

4

If you were talking with a seeker who had never stepped foot into a church, how would you explain what God has done to show His love for them?

5

When did you first really experience the depth of God's sacrificial love for you, and what helped you to understand it?

Read Snapshot "The Presence of the Holy Spirit"

THE PRESENCE OF THE HOLY SPIRIT

Not only does God tell us that we matter to Him, but He also proves His love by His actions. One of the things God has done to show us His love is to send the Holy Spirit to live inside of us. The Holy Spirit assumes the full-time task of warming up your heart and making you a more relational, tender, loving person. When God puts His Holy Spirit in your life, it's like turning a spotlight on a cold, hard heart. The Holy Spirit starts melting you, tenderizing you, making you soft toward God and people. And the good news is that the Holy Spirit will continue to work in you for the rest of your life!

6 How have you experienced the transforming presence and power of the Holy Spirit in the following areas of your life:

- How you love family members

- How you love and care for other followers of Christ

- How you feel toward those who do not yet know God's love

7 What are some of the things you do that limit the impact of the Holy Spirit's power in your life?

What can you do to give the Holy Spirit greater control and room to work in your life?

Read Snapshot "A New Community"

A NEW COMMUNITY

Like it or not, we are deeply impacted by those with whom we spend time. If we are around people who are filled with hate and anger, that hate and anger will eventually begin to infect us. If we are in a community filled with people who know how to love each other, this will also have a transforming effect on our lives. When we become followers of Christ, God places us in a loving community where we are surrounded by people who are diligently seeking to become better at loving.

---

8 If there is a person who is having a negative influence on your life and faith, what can you do to limit their ability to impact your life?

What needs to change in your schedule so that you can spend more time in community with other followers of Christ?

9

Picture someone in your life who would benefit from an expression of love from you. What will you do to express your love, and how can the group keep you accountable to this commitment?

PUTTING YOURSELF IN THE PICTURE

You Matter to God

Take time in the coming week to identify two people who need encouragement. Commit yourself to either call them on the phone, write them a letter, or meet with them. Let your primary concern be to communicate to them how much they matter to God. Remind them of what God has done to show His love for them and what Jesus has done to extend forgiveness to them. Also, communicate your love and care for them. Let them know they matter to God and they matter to you.

Growing in Community

Think of one follower of Christ you know personally who has stopped participating in regular times of worship and Christian community. Contact that person in the coming week and invite them to join you for some kind of gathering of believers.

What changes can you make to create more opportunities for Christian community? Is there an opportunity for deeper fellowship you are not taking advantage of? Spending time with other followers of Christ is essential for our own spiritual growth. What can you do in the coming month to deepen your commitment to developing Christian community?

TENDER LOVE

REFLECTIONS FROM SESSION 1

1. If you took time since your last small group meeting to contact a person for the purpose of reminding them that they matter to God, tell your group about this experience. How did they respond to your "Good News"? How did you feel when you reminded them how much they matter to God?

2. If you made a commitment to work at growing in Christian community, how are you doing at keeping your commitment? If you have been developing more opportunities for community with other followers of Christ, how has this been impacting your desire to express love?

THE BIG PICTURE

It certainly seems to be a whole lot easier for some people to be tenderhearted than it does for others. Tenderness seems to be sort of a reflex reaction to some people, while for others it seems to be foreign and difficult.

Many years ago we experienced the truth of this in our own home. A huge plant in a room of our house got a disease. My wife was worried about the disease spreading to other plants in the house, so she decided that she would have to cut the plant down and dispose of it. She hacked all the branches down, put them in some garbage bags, and left the big pot and the stump of the plant right there in the room so that when I got home I could carry it out to the garage.

Later in the afternoon both of our kids came home. They burst into the room and saw where that huge houseplant used to be. My son, who was six years old at the time, burst into tears and asked Lynne why she had done such an awful thing. Why did she have to *kill* the plant? Did it hurt when the plant was killed? Did it bleed? Couldn't she have called a doctor? He was just broken over the event. He was tenderhearted then and he still is today. It took about a half an hour for Lynne to put him all back together again and explain why she had cut down the plant.

Our daughter was nine years old at the time, and she had an entirely different response. She said with disgust, "It was only a sick old houseplant. Don't worry about it. I'm glad mom chopped it down and put it out of its misery." She said, "Are you going to chop down any more, Mom? Do you need any help?"

Two children, born of the same parents, raised in the same family, in the same house, with the same levels of love. However, one is a lot more tender than the other.

A WIDE ANGLE VIEW

1 Tell about a person in your life who is very tender-hearted. How does their tenderness help them express love in a way that touches the lives of others?

A BIBLICAL PORTRAIT

Ephesians 4:29–32

2 What does this passage call us to be and what does it warn us to avoid?

How might following the teachings of this passage impact the life of a Christian?

3 What one item listed in the passage (something to seek or something to get rid of) needs work in your life?

What can your group members do to help you grow in this area?

SHARPENING THE FOCUS

Read Snapshot "Tough-Hearted People"

TOUGH-HEARTED PEOPLE

It's time for us tough-hearted people to be honest. We do a lot more damage to people than we think we do, don't we? We kid people whom we shouldn't kid, saying, "Can't they take a joke?" when they act hurt. We think it's their problem, but it's really ours.

We also don't listen to people all that well. Often, while others are talking to us, we are either making different plans or planning a response to what they're saying. We don't have that natural, built-in sensitivity that others possess.

We really wonder why most folks are so weak and timid. We even occasionally use people, disposing of them unceremoniously when they've served our purposes. We walk with an air of superiority. We love to be right. We naturally compete. We have a deep need to win, and we tend to keep ourselves very busy. If the truth were known, sometimes we view tenderhearted people as emotional weaklings or psychological misfits. We don't understand them.

4 If you consider yourself a tenderhearted person, how do you react to the portrait of a tough-hearted person in the above Snapshot?

If you consider yourself a tough-hearted person, how do you react to this portrayal? Why do you think you react this way?

Read Snapshot "A New Look at People"

A NEW LOOK AT PEOPLE

God is ready to give us some loving lessons today—understandable, practical, positive lessons. He wants us to know how a tough-hearted person can become more tender. If you really want that to happen, then slow down, take a closer look at the people around you, and try to see them for who they really are. What would your day be like if you saw people through God's eyes? Here's a person who is a custom-designed creation of the Almighty God. Here is a person who has God's very image stamped on her. Here is a person who is the object of God's greatest affection. Here is a person for whom Jesus shed His blood. Here is a person the Holy Spirit is seeking out night and day in order to bring him to a relationship with the Father. Here is a person who is God's greatest treasure. Here is a person who really matters to God.

If you view people like obstacles on the landscape to avoid or manage, you need a new perspective. If people don't particularly mean a whole lot to you, it's time to look at them from God's point of view. You need your vision changed. You need a new understanding of who people are.

---

5 Place an empty chair in the middle of your group and imagine you have a tough-hearted, insensitive person sitting in it. Take time as a group to talk about how you might counsel this person in the following areas:

- The damage that can be done when they treat people like a part of the landscape or furniture rather than a living, breathing, feeling child of God.
- The way they make people feel when they treat them with tough-hearted insensitivity.
- How they can learn to see people as God sees them.

Read Snapshot "Slow Down"

SLOW DOWN

Tough-hearted people tend to be on the fast track. They're going places. They're getting things done. Their adrenaline starts pumping. They have goals to achieve and quotas to meet and deadlines and budgets and deals to cut. To a tough-hearted, fast-track person, people are either tools to be used or trouble to be avoided. And so tough-hearted people say things like, "Well, she's a winner, but he's a loser. She's a heavyweight; he's a lightweight. She's sharp; she's two bricks short of a load. He's a survivor; he's a basket case." You see, tough-hearted people tend to view other people in comparison to themselves and their own projects and aspirations, as opposed to seeing people for who they really are in God's eyes.

6 When you get pulled into a fast-paced, driven lifestyle, how does this impact the way you view and treat the following people:

- Family members

- Friends

- Colleagues in the marketplace

- Those who don't yet know God's love

7   If you are on the fast track right now, what needs to happen for you to slow down and get a new perspective on life and people?

How can your group members help you slow down and keep you accountable to live a slower-paced life?

Read Snapshot "Walking in Their Shoes"

WALKING IN THEIR SHOES

Another way a tough-hearted person can become more tender is to take a few moments to "walk a mile in another person's shoes." That saying comes from an old Indian proverb about walking in someone else's moccasins. Tenderhearted people have a tendency to do that naturally. But tough-hearted people can look at those who are hurting, broken, and upset and just shoot right on by. They rarely stop and say, "I wonder what it feels like to be in their situation?" If we learn to slow down and look at life from the perspective of others, we will discover that a softening process begins to happen naturally.

---

8   What would the people in your life learn about you if they could walk in your shoes for a whole week?

Read Snapshot "WWJD?"

Another way to grow in tenderheartedness is to ask the very simple question, "What would Jesus do?" Think about it. If Jesus is our model for all of life, then He is certainly the best one to follow as we seek to grow in love with others. How would Jesus respond or care? What would Jesus say to this person? What tone of voice would Jesus use? We need to ask this question often if we are going to grow more tender in the way we relate to others.

9 Tell the group about a person in your life with whom you have a difficult time being tender. Allow other group members to communicate how they think Jesus would respond toward this person in this situation.

PUTTING YOURSELF IN THE PICTURE

BRINGING DOWN THE RPMs

What specific things can you do in the coming weeks to slow down the pace of your life and get a new look at the people around you? Who will pray for you and encourage you as you slow down the RPMs of your daily schedule?

TAKING YOUR ADVICE

Your group members gave you their perspective on how they feel Jesus would respond to a specific person in your life. Pray about the counsel and advice they gave you and see if some of it is helpful as you seek to grow more tender toward this person in your daily interactions. What actions will you take in the coming days to treat this person more like Jesus would treat them?

TOUGH LOVE

REFLECTIONS FROM SESSION 2

1. What have you been doing to try to slow down the pace of your life? If you are being successful in slowing down the RPMs, how is this bringing refreshment and making you more able to feel and express love?

2. If you took advice from a group member on how to tenderly care for a person in your life, how did this advice work? Would you recommend it to others?

THE BIG PICTURE

Who said the following words: "Woe to you, teachers of the law and Pharisees, you hypocrites! You are like whitewashed tombs, which look beautiful on the outside but on the inside are full of dead man's bones and everything unclean." Or "In the same way, on the outside you appear to people as righteous but on the inside you are full of hypocrisy and wickedness." Or "You snakes! You brood of vipers! How will you escape being condemned to hell?" Or "I tell you the truth, no one can enter the kingdom of God unless he is born of water and the Spirit."

Who was it that said all of these hard, hard words? Of course, most of you know. It was Jesus Christ, the Son of God.

Why? you ask. Why would the gentle Shepherd, the tender-hearted, meek, and lowly Savior say tough words like these? Why would he talk so strongly to people He claimed to love? Why did He say all of those harsh things?

I think there are two main reasons. First, Jesus spoke tough words because they were true. The words were hard. They were upsetting. They were difficult to receive and tough to swallow. But they were true. Quite often the truth must be told in a straightforward and clear manner. Sometimes there needs to be no room left for confusion or misinterpretation.

The second reason was that He had an overwhelming concern for the people He was addressing. He was absorbed in the well-being of people. And so, from time to time, He had to take off the gloves, roll up His sleeves, and force people to come to grips with some things before they shipwrecked their lives and jeopardized their eternities.

A WIDE ANGLE VIEW

1 Tell about a situation when you had to speak hard words to someone for their own good (a child, parent, sibling, friend, or coworker). How did you feel when you did this?

Can you remember a time when someone had to speak tough words to you for your own good? How did it feel to have someone speak to you this way?

A BIBLICAL PORTRAIT

Read Ephesians 4:14–16

2 This passage draws a vivid contrast between those who are spiritual infants, tossed around by various teachings and false doctrines, and those who are mature enough to speak the truth in love.

How does "speaking the truth in love" do the following things:

- Show that we are no longer infants in the faith

- Help us grow closer in our relationship with Jesus

- Strengthen the body of Christ (the church)

SHARPENING THE FOCUS

Read Snapshot "The Need for Balance"

THE NEED FOR BALANCE

I believe with all my heart that there is not enough tough love being expressed these days. There is certainly a need for tender love in this world. We need compassion, sensitivity, affirmation, and encouragement. But tender love without its counterpart—tough love—can rapidly degenerate into a sniveling kind of sentimentality that paves the way for deception and the eventual disintegration of relationships. If you have only tender love in a relationship, that relationship is eventually headed for trouble. If it's not balanced with tough love, the tender love will eventually mean very little. These words need to be heard especially by those of you who are by nature a little more tenderhearted. Tough love may be foreign to you. It may seem unnatural and even a little bit frightening. And some of you might even think it's unbiblical. But guess what? It's just as biblical as tender love. The key is balance!

3

What are some possible consequences when a person expresses *only tender love* when:

- Raising children

- Communicating with a spouse

29

- Relating with coworkers

- Building a friendship

What are some possible consequences when a person expresses only tough love when:

- Raising children

- Communicating with a spouse

- Relating with coworkers

- Building a friendship

Read Sidenote "Truth-telling vs. Peacekeeping"

TRUTH-TELLING VS. PEACEKEEPING

Truth-telling is more important than peacekeeping. Also, the well-being of the other person is far more important than the current comfort level in our relationship. However, there is often a little voice that says, "Don't tell the truth. Remain silent, keep the peace and the problem will just go away." Friends, that kind of peace is a form of deception from the pit of hell. When there's tension building in a relationship and you know what needs to be said, it's the Evil One who will say to you, "Don't tell the truth. He won't listen to it. She won't receive it. It will blow up in your face. It will cause too much hurt. It will only make things worse. It will cause all kinds of upheaval, anxiety, and turmoil." And on and on go the lies. If you get sucked into that deception and choose peacekeeping over truth-telling, there's a high probability that you will kill the relationship sooner or later. It's a counterfeit peace—a relationship built on deception.

4 Why are we so often tempted to "swallow the truth" and "keep the peace" rather than tell the truth?

What consequences have you experienced in your own life and relationships when you have decided to "keep peace" rather than tell the truth?

Read Snapshot "Whose Well-being?"

WHOSE WELL-BEING?

Imagine a mother sitting in her kitchen watching her three-year-old boy out riding his Big Wheel in the driveway. He's having a great time. Her heart just spills over with love. It's a hot day so she runs and gets a big cold cup of lemonade for him. She goes outdoors and picks up the little guy and hugs him and says how much she loves him. She gives him the lemonade, and as she watches him drink it there is a tenderness and warmth that goes beyond words. She goes back into the house to put the cup away. The child gets back on his Big Wheel and cruises right out into the street, where he has been told never to ride. The mother sees it, comes flying out the door, picks up the little kid, and suddenly has a totally different look on her face and tone in her voice than she had just two minutes earlier. She takes him into the house, gives him a stern lecture on safety, and disciplines him.

At that moment that mother is living in the dynamic tension of tender love and tough love. She is saying, "This is not the time for warm fuzzies. Now we're dealing with life-and-death issues, and it's time for tough love." The well-being of that little boy is far more important than warm fuzzies.

5

Why is consistent truth-telling one of the greatest indications of a truly loving relationship?

6

It would be nice to think that every time we exercise tough love we would receive a warm thank-you card and a box of chocolates. However, life does not always work that way. What was a time you spoke the truth in love and met resistance or even hostility?

What did you do to seek healing in this relationship without compromising the truth?

Read Snapshot "Opening Pandora's Box"

OPENING PANDORA'S BOX

If these loving lessons are what they are cracked up to be, they're going to have to create some tension in your own life. That means it's time to open Pandora's box. Who are you choosing to keep the peace with instead of telling the truth? Is it a husband, wife, son, daughter, employer, employee, parent, pastor, friend? Whoever you are doing that with, you are hurting them. You're cheating yourself, them, and God. What does God's Word say for you to do? It says to stop lying. Stop this counterfeit peace. Trust God. Pray. Go gently and sit down with the person and say, "I want to confess something to you. I have lead you to believe all along that there is peace in this relationship. But I've been lying to you about something. I am not satisfied with this. Before it poisons this relationship any further, I want to tell you about it. How can we work this out?"

7

Who is one person you need to meet with and speak the truth in love?

How can your group members pray for you and support you in your commitment to speak the truth in love with this person?

PUTTING YOURSELF IN THE PICTURE

STRIKING A BALANCE

Who is one person to whom you tend to express tender love but need to grow in the area of tough love? What can you do in the coming weeks to strike a balance in this relationship?

Who is one person to whom you tend to express tough love but need to grow in the area of tender love? What can you do in the coming weeks to strike a balance in this relationship?

As a group, how can you express tender or tough love to one another?

GROWING UP IN CHRIST

The apostle Paul is clear that speaking the truth is a sign of maturity in Christ. Take time in the coming week to memorize the following verse. Let these words impact the way you relate to others:

Instead, speaking the truth in love, we will in all things grow up into him who is the Head, that is, Christ (Eph. 4:15).

SACRIFICIAL LOVE

REFLECTIONS FROM SESSION 3

1. If you took time since your last small group meeting to express tender or tough love, tell your group about this experience. Particularly, if you tried to express a kind of love that does not come as naturally to you, how did it feel to express love in a way that does not naturally fall in your comfort zone?

2. If you memorized Ephesians 4:15, quote it for your group and tell them what you feel it means.

THE BIG PICTURE

People say a lot of strange things about love. They say that love is a many-splendored thing. To be honest, I've never understood what that meant. One popular song says that love is like a rose. People also say that love is a free-flowing feeling of benevolence and good will toward all people—that sounds like a Christmas card to me. I have even heard it said that love is a scintillating opportunity to meet someone's need, which will result in miraculous bonds of mutuality, lifelong respect, and admiration.

Scenario #1—A Parable of Love. If I were to tell the parable of the Good Samaritan in light of today's popularized, mushy kind of love, it would read something like this: Imagine the Good Samaritan driving on a country road in his new convertible with the top down and the wind blowing in his hair. Suddenly he sees a beautiful blond standing alongside of her red Porsche waving a lace handkerchief. Thinking she must have a flat tire, the Good Samaritan says to himself, "I feel a surge of desire to assist this woman with her flat tire." He pulls off to the side of the road, introduces himself, easily locates the jack, and changes the tire without ever looking confused or getting his hands dirty. Meanwhile the woman is standing nearby, complementing the Good Samaritan's marvelous skill and strength. When the job is done, the car is lowered to the ground and the jack is put away. The damsel in distress reaches into her purse, pulls out five, crisp, one-hundred-dollar bills and places them in the Good Samaritan's hand. She then plants a kiss on his cheek and says, "I don't know how I can thank you enough," and speeds off in her Porsche. The Good Samaritan puts the $500 in his wallet, and drives away in the moonlight smiling and singing "Love is a many-splendored thing."

Scenario #2—Love in the Real World. When we seek to follow the example of sacrificial love modeled in the story of the Good Samaritan, it is usually not as romantic as we might hope. It was a twenty-degree-below zero January day and I was driving home from my workout at the "Y." I saw a middle-aged women with a dirty little Toyota pulled off in the snowbank on the side of the road. To be honest, I fully intended to pass her by. I had things to do and people to see and places to go, and I had wet hair and no hat and no gloves and I was wearing deck shoes. But I felt a convicting voice of the Holy Spirit saying, "Love." And I said, "What did I do to deserve instructions like this? It's twenty below. It's a dirty little Toyota. It's a middle-aged woman." But I turned around and went back.

That choice started a comedy of errors. Her trunk was full of books and clothes, and I couldn't find the jack. When I finally found the jack, I couldn't figure out how to work it. By this time it was getting dark, and she was holding a little flashlight and reading the owner's manual to me. The temperature seemed to keep dropping. When I finally figured out how to work the jack, I discovered my hands were stuck to it. When I finally got the car off the ground, I discovered there was no lug wrench in the trunk. We had to drive three blocks to a friend's house. She went in for hot chocolate, and I stayed out and finished the job. She came out warm, and thanked me. She then drove off into the dark, and I've never seen her again. I managed to get my frostbitten body into the car, and drove home saying to myself, as my brain thawed out, "Where is this rose that they talk about? Where is this many-splendored thing?"

A WIDE ANGLE VIEW

1 What picture of love and life does each of the scenarios paint?

What are the contrasts between these two pictures of love?

A BIBLICAL PORTRAIT

Read John 3:16–17 and 1 John 4:9–12

2 What are some of the things God has done to show His love for you?

In light of the way God loves us, how would you define true love?

Read Snapshot "A Worldly Perspective"

A WORLDLY PERSPECTIVE

We live in a culture that teaches selfishness rather than self-sacrifice. We are constantly bombarded with books, radio shows, television programs, magazine articles, and newspaper articles that shout "protect your time!" Culture urges us to conserve our time so that we can have more of it for ourselves, to conserve our energy so that when we get some leisure time, we have energy to expend on ourselves. Our culture says to accumulate resources, amass them, stockpile them, invest them, double them, triple them so that we have more at our disposal. We have had those values drummed into our minds so much over the course of our lives that it's impossible to live in the culture without being affected by them.

3

What are the primary messages and values promoted by our culture today?

If you were to write a billboard that summarizes the central message of the media, what would it say?

Read Snapshot "True Gratification"

TRUE GRATIFICATION

True fulfillment in life will never come through self-gratification. It will never come from protecting yourself and pleasing yourself and hoarding things for yourself. That's a dead-end road. True fulfillment comes when you give yourself to God and to the service of His people. We have to make a choice. Every day, many times a day, we are going to come to crossroads that afford us rich opportunities to love people, to expend our time, energy, and resources for them. What will we do with these opportunities? It is only when we decide to live lives filled with sacrificial love that we discover true and lasting gratification. As strange and backward as it seems, the more we give of ourselves and our resources, the richer we become. We discover that joy and gratification come only through sacrificial love.

4

Who comes to mind when you think of sacrificial love?

How have you seen the love of Jesus through this person's life?

Read Snapshot "Sacrificial Love in Marriage"

SACRIFICIAL LOVE IN MARRIAGE

 I realize that some members of your group may not be married, but this intimate relationship is certainly a central testing ground for sacrificial love. When it comes to marital love, the world says each spouse should look out for their own needs, making sure that each is getting the best out of the relationship. The key is to make sure the marriage isn't costing us anything or inhibiting us from doing the things we want or keeping us from experiencing our full potential in life. But God has other plans for those who marry. He calls us to serve our spouse and to think of their needs, desires, and dreams as even more important than our own. Pretty radical stuff!

5

Why is sacrificial love an essential element of any healthy marriage?

What happens in a marriage when one or both parties begin to focus only on their own needs, desires, and dreams?

Read Snapshot "Sacrificial Love in Friendships?"

SACRIFICIAL LOVE IN FRIENDSHIPS

The world doesn't begin to understand the concept of brotherhood and sisterhood. It says to find some like-minded, like-incomed people who vote like you and have about the same handicap in golf. Some nice, *safe* people. And then you keep a healthy detachment from them so that the relationship doesn't get muddied up with commitments or expectations. You relate with them at a safe distance over a period of time. That works out all right until you experience a pressing problem—a loss, a tragedy, a death, an illness. And suddenly the realization comes crashing in on you that no one really cares much about you, your life, or your problems. Your friendships are based on convenient love, not sacrificial love.

The Bible tells us to find a few brothers and sisters and decide at the outset to expend yourself for them. You're going to take time and make time to be together regularly. You are going to talk deeply about life and faith and seek to build each other up. You're going to let the waters get muddy and get into each other's lives, encouraging, counseling, challenging, and rebuking each other. You're going to open up your resources to one another and be willing to share what you have. That's right, you will give away what the world tells you to cling to if you see a friend in need. If you approach your friendships with this kind of mind-set, watch what happens to the quality of your relationships. See what happens when you decide to show sacrificial love in relationships.

6 What are the marks of a friendship built on mutual, sacrificial love?

How can you develop these characteristics in your friendships?

7 In what area of your life do you see yourself holding back love and not being willing to give sacrificially?

PUTTING YOURSELF IN THE PICTURE

LEARNING FROM THE MASTER

Jesus is our ultimate example of sacrificial love. He gave His life for us. He left the glory of heaven, lived a perfect life on this earth, and died on a cross so that we could know the love of the Father. Take time in the coming days to think about how Jesus has shown you sacrificial love. Think about the following questions as you learn about sacrificial love from the Master.

- What did Jesus leave and sacrifice when He came from the glory of heaven and lived on this earth?
- What sacrifices did Jesus make during His life of ministry and His sacrifice on the cross?

As you think about and meditate on all the sacrifices Jesus has made for you, pray for strength and commitment to be more sacrificial in the way you extend love to others.

SACRIFICIAL GOALS

Identify one person in your life who you need to love more sacrificially. It may be a spouse, a child, a friend, a coworker, or any number of people. Identify one specific way you will show that person love in the coming week. Allow yourself to move beyond your own comfort zone and be creative in terms of what you will sacrifice. You may want to have a friend pray for you and keep you accountable to follow through on your goal.

STEADFAST LOVE

REFLECTIONS FROM SESSION 4

1. How has reflecting on the sacrificial life and death of Jesus impacted your commitment to live a life filled with sacrificial love?
2. If you took time to extend sacrificial love to someone over the past week, what impact did this act of love have on them?

THE BIG PICTURE

Like most sons, I suppose, I didn't receive many letters from my father when I was growing up. When he traveled, which he did extensively, he would make long-distance phone calls now and then. When I would go to summer camp or on some other trip, my mom usually handled the letter-writing responsibilities. However, every once in a while, when he was on an extended business trip or when I had been away at college for several months, I would get a letter from my dad. To be honest, I don't remember much of the content of those letters. What I do remember is the way he closed his letters to me. Without fail, the last line of his letters to me said the same thing: *"Remember to love those people who need love the most. Dad."*

You have to understand, my dad was a man's man. He was a regular kind of guy. He liked to watch Matt Dillan and "The Untouchables" and things like that. You would think he would close his letter like many dads close letters to their sons. "Don't do anything that I wouldn't do, Son." But what few letters I received from my dad all ended with that same phrase. "Love those people who need love the most."

If you had known my dad, you would know he had every right in the world to issue that challenge. He had a lot of idiosyncrasies, faults, and problems like the rest of us. But his life

43

was a testimony to that phrase. In spite of all of his business activities, for twenty-five years on Sunday afternoons, he would lead a little hymn sing and Bible study for about a hundred mentally-retarded women at the Kalamazoo State Hospital in Michigan. He would even change his travel itinerary to get home from wherever he was during the week so he could meet with those dear women.

When the Vietnamese refugee situation bombarded this country, he adopted four or five families, brought them to Kalamazoo, and secured housing for them. He found them jobs and cars and things like that. He also helped rebuild a type of mission house for vagrants in downtown Kalamazoo. He helped handicapped people start businesses. I remember the time he helped a blind man start a restaurant. I kept saying, "Dad, I don't know if that's going to work." And he said, "Well, let's give it a shot." My dad earned the right to challenge me and others to "Love those who need love the most," because he did it himself for many, many years.

A WIDE ANGLE VIEW

1 Who in your life has been an example and model of steadfast love?

How has their example of steadfast love marked your life?

A BIBLICAL PORTRAIT

Read 1 Samuel 30:6

2 What do you think it means to find strength in the Lord?

Why is this so difficult to do for so many of us?

SHARPENING THE FOCUS

3 If you compare your ability to feel and express love to a fuel tank, how full is your tank right now? Mark the graph below to reflect how full your tank is at this time in your life.

Empty   Low   Half full   Full   Overflowing

If your tank is low, what is depleting your source of love?

If your tank is full, what is keeping you fueled up?

If your tank is half full, what needs to happen to fill it up?

Read Snapshot "A Triangle of Steadfastness"

A TRIANGLE OF STEADFASTNESS

Since my father's death I have tried to follow in his footsteps when it comes to loving those people who need love the most. To be honest, I have failed more than I have succeeded. However, I have continued to try to be steadfast and face the challenges that have come my way. I have actually put my thoughts on this topic into a three-part personal challenge about steadfast loving. I have rephrased my father's challenge a little bit. This is how I put it:

- Love those who are difficult to love.
- Love even when it is difficult for you to be loving.
- Love without looking for anything back in return.

These three goals act as a triangle of steadfastness that challenge me in my daily life of faith.

Who are the people you have the hardest time loving? Why?

Read Snapshot "Empty and Angry"

EMPTY AND ANGRY

Some of us have a strong moral fiber. We say, "I'm just going to keep on going. Even though I'm all out of love, I'm just going to press on." What tends to happen is that we come to a point where we wind up being both empty and angry. Angry at the very people that we ought to be loving. Angry at people who matter to God. Angry at His most precious treasure. We drain ourselves to the point where people become problems to be avoided. When the phone rings, we stiffen, viewing the call as an intrusion. Each note or a letter we receive just represents another need, another obligation to which we must respond. And when unexpected guests drop by our homes, we see them as invading our privacy.

5

Tell about a time you felt empty and angry because your supply of love was depleted.

What helped you refuel your tanks and recapture a joy for life and desire to love others?

Read Snapshot "Refueling Your Spiritual Tank"

REFUELING YOUR SPIRITUAL TANK

When the pressure got to be too much, David left the crowds, the demands, and all of his serving opportunities. He took a time out. He went back to the basics, getting away by himself so he could have a long talk with God. He poured himself out to the Lord. He reminded himself of God's promises, of God's love and His willingness to help. In a way, David took a time out to bask a little while in God's love for him. He had to remember that he mattered to God. That he was a child of God.

Jesus did the same thing. After many long bouts of loving and serving people, leading and counseling and teaching people, He would leave the multitudes and go into the mountains to pray. Sometimes He would cross the Sea of Galilee to replenish Himself with conversations with the Father. It goes without saying that if people like David and Jesus needed to go and replenish themselves spiritually, so do we!

6

What are some of the things you do to fill up your spiritual tank?

What depletes your tank? How do you avoid these things?

Read Snapshot "Refueling Your Emotional Tank"

REFUELING YOUR EMOTIONAL TANK

There is another gauge that you have to watch in this business of loving people over the long haul—your emotional fuel gauge. Believe it or not, you can keep your spiritual reserves replenished and still feel like you are all out of love. If this happens, it may be because you have depleted your emotional reserves. You can be enjoying great fellowship with God and still have no real desire to love people because emotionally you are on empty. The two main things experts say help us stay fresh emotionally are relaxation and recreation. If we make time for these, we will keep our tanks full. If we neglect them, we are asking for trouble.

7 What do you do for relaxation and recreation to keep yourself emotionally fueled up?

What do you need to avoid that depletes your emotional tank?

Read Snapshot "Keeping Your Physical Tank Full"

KEEPING YOUR PHYSICAL TANK FULL

There is one more gauge you have to watch. That's your physical gauge. What happens to your relationships when you get run down physically? You know what happens. A war starts, or the relationships start to die from neglect. I've discovered that there are multitudes of people wandering around these days who are run down physically. Most of them have no idea how much this undermines their attempts at loving other people. They don't realize that it takes energy—not only spiritual and emotional energy, but also physical energy—to really serve someone. People who are physically run down just can't summon that kind of energy. And people who are run down tend to be easily irritated, critical, short-fused, defensive, and negative. We need to keep our physical tanks fueled up if we are going to be steadfast in loving others.

8 What habits must change if you are going to be more effective at keeping your physical tank filled?

What can your group members do to support and encourage you in this area of your life?

9 If we are going to be steadfast in our love and care for others over the long haul, we need to learn to read the gauges of our lives and be sure our tanks don't run too low. Using the charts below, take a moment to review the three areas we have discussed. Where would you say your fuel gauge is in each area?

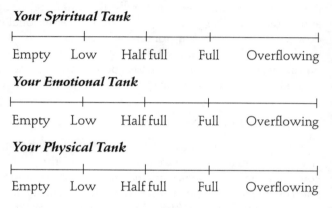

Your Spiritual Tank

Empty   Low   Half full   Full   Overflowing

Your Emotional Tank

Empty   Low   Half full   Full   Overflowing

Your Physical Tank

Empty   Low   Half full   Full   Overflowing

Which area is lowest in your life right now, and what do you need to do to get refueled in this area?

Which area is strongest, and what can you do to be an encouragement to others in this area?

SPIRITUAL REFUELING

If you do not have a regular habit of spending time with God, commit yourself to a time of Bible study and prayer each day. It can be in the morning, evening, or at your lunch break. The time of day is not as important as the fact that you are spending time with God each day. Just being in His presence will help refuel your tank.

EMOTIONAL REFUELING

For some people this comes naturally. For others, relaxation and recreation is like pulling teeth. If you feel emotionally run down, block out some time for fun and recreation in the coming week. If you don't have any hobbies or things you do for fun, find some. Contact a friend who is good at relaxing and playing and ask them to take you out and teach you how to relax!

PHYSICAL REFUELING

If you are out of shape, have bad eating habits, fail to get enough sleep on a regular basis, or treat your body poorly in any way, commit yourself to break some bad habits and begin some good ones. This is one area where encouragement and accountability from friends is essential. Ask a friend to support you as you develop new habits in caring for your physical health.

RADICAL LOVE

REFLECTIONS FROM SESSION 5

1. What have you been doing since your last small group meeting to keep your spiritual tank full? Is there anything your group members can do to be an encouragement in this are of your life?
2. What have you been doing in the past weeks for emotional refreshment? What are you doing to be sure you have adequate recreation and relaxation time?
3. If you set goals for you personal physical health, how are you doing in meeting these goals? If you are keeping your commitments in this area of your life, how are you using your renewed energy to extend love to others?

THE BIG PICTURE

The scene is a mountainside overlooking a beautiful inland lake. Jesus was ready to deliver what many people say was the most astounding sermon in history. You probably know it as the Sermon on the Mount. The Sermon on the Mount begins with the Beatitudes and then extends to cover a wide variety of topics. One of these topics is love. However, the Beatitudes contains no ordinary teaching on love. If we consider the past five lessons on love in this series a college level course on loving, this teaching of Jesus is an advanced Ph. D. course. It is about radical love.

I think that as Jesus came to this part of the Sermon on the Mount, He was determined to force His followers to take the next step in their understanding of radical Christian love. I think He was saying, "Friends, you are making reasonable progress in understanding the essence of the Christian faith. But when it comes to understanding the quality of inter-personal relationships I want you to have, you need some straightforward, practical, eye-opening information. So listen closely to a few down-to-earth, everyday illustrations of what I am talking about when I challenge you to become involved in demonstrating radical love."

Jesus asked them to imagine what it would feel like to have someone square off in front of them and then give them a backhanded slap across their face. In that culture, a backhanded slap was considered the ultimate act of degradation. Even in our culture today, when we are insulted, we say, "Well, that was a real slap across the face."

Jesus wanted them to think long and hard about how they would respond to this slap in the face. It's as if He is saying, "What are you going to do? You can still feel the sting of the slap across your face. Your adrenaline is flowing. Your anger level is skyrocketing. Your honor is at stake. You know you could knock this guy into the middle of next week if you wanted to. And there are voices inside of you saying, 'Hit him back.'"

Jesus is saying, "Here's the moment of truth. What are you going to do? I say from here on out, the thing to do is to demonstrate a new kind of love. Radical love. Don't slap him back. Don't scream at him. Don't curse him under your breath. Look at the man straight in the eye and remind yourself that even in spite of this man's arrogance and anger, he matters to God. Even at this very moment, God is trying to reach out to that guy. So dig down deep into the foundations of your faith and love him. Do something radical that will mark his life. If turning the other cheek for a second slap will make a mark on the man's soul, turn the other cheek. There is tremendous power in radical, nonretaliatory love."

A WIDE ANGLE VIEW

1 How have you been the recipient of radical love?

How can you express radical love? To whom?

A BIBLICAL PORTRAIT

Read Matthew 5:38–42

This short passage contains four illustrations of radical
love. What are these illustrations and how can each be
lived out in our day and culture?

3 Respond to the two statements below: ·

*"These verses must be taken absolutely literally. As
Christians, we must take all abuse without questioning, give
away everything we have upon request, and serve everyone
who asks."*

*"This passage can't be taken seriously. Jesus could not have
meant what He seems to be saying. This teaching of Jesus
does not call us to suffer abuse or give away our possessions.
It is more an encouragement to have a thoughtful and kind
spirit toward others."*

SHARPENING THE FOCUS

Read Snapshot "Outrageous Giving"

OUTRAGEOUS GIVING

Jesus also told His followers, "If you make a deal with somebody and you can't come through with your end of the bargain, be ready to give even more than the law requires. For example, if the person demands your *inner garment* as overnight collateral, then you have to give it to him ... it's the law." But I say to you, "Stand in front of him and offer him your *outer garment*, your blanket. Look him straight in the eye and say, 'I know by civil law I am permitted to keep my outer garment for my blanket tonight, but maybe you or one of your children or servants could use my robe tonight. I'll get by somehow. Take it. And by the way, is there anything else that you need of mine? Any other service that I can render to your family? I would be happy to do that too.'"

You see, Jesus is saying radical love oftentimes exceeds the limits of any written law. Radical love doesn't seek to get away with doing the barest minimum. Radical love goes far beyond the minimum—it gets outrageous.

4 How can outrageous giving be a sign of radical love?

How has God modeled this practice of outrageous giving in your life?

Read Snapshot "Going the Extra Mile"

GOING THE EXTRA MILE

Jesus told His followers how to respond when a Roman soldier pulled them off the street and made them carry his luggage (the law permitted Roman soldiers to do this). Jesus said, "When you get to the end of the one-mile limit, instead of slamming the trunk or the suitcase to the ground, hoping to break something fragile on the inside, demonstrate radical love. When you get to the end of that mile, say, 'Sir, could I be of further service to you in anyway? You matter so much to the Father that it would be a privilege for me to be able to serve someone so special in His sight. If you want to go another mile, I'll go with you. If you want to ask me some questions along the way, feel free. Let's go another mile together. I would be happy to do that for you." Jesus said, "Try that. That's nonretaliatory, second-mile love. You'll be amazed at the mark you can make on people's lives through such radical love."

5 What are some of the practical ways you can go above and beyond the call of duty in the following areas of your life:

- Among family members

- At your place of employment

- At church

- In relationships with seekers

What impact do you hope to have by making it a habit to do some of these "extra-mile" acts of love?

6 What one specific "extra-mile" goal will you set for the coming weeks?

How can your group members pray for you and support you in this commitment?

Read Snapshot "Why Such Radical Love?"

WHY SUCH RADICAL LOVE?

God knows there are some situations and people who call for a special level of radical love. There are three reasons why this kind of extra-mile love is needed. First, in a hostile and violent world, those with nonretaliatory love can break the cycle of interpersonal hostility. Second, in a hard-hearted world, those with second-mile love have the potential to make a mark on the lives of men and women who could not be reached any other way. And third, when we extend this kind of radical love, our souls are knit to the heart of God because He knows all about this kind of love.

Do you want to be part of God's solution to the violence and hostility in this world? Show radical love! Do you want to help reach people who matter to God, but whose hearts are too hard to realize it? Extend radical love! Do you want your soul to be closely knit with the heart of God? Learn to love radically, just as Jesus did. Your life will never be the same.

7

How have you seen God's love triumph over hostility and violence?

8

Who is one person you know who is hard-hearted to the love of God?

What can you do to show this person radical love when you see them?

9

How have you seen your heart knit to the heart of God as you have tried to be a person who shows radical love?

PUTTING YOURSELF IN THE PICTURE

EXTRA-MILE LOVE

Who is one person you want to love by going above and beyond the call of duty? It may be a family member, a friend, a seeker, or someone at work. Set a specific goal for how you will extend radical love to this person.

What will you do?

When will you do it?

Who will pray for you and keep you accountable?

TURNING THE OTHER CHEEK

Take time in the coming week to memorize the following passage from Matthew. Pray for a deeper understanding of what it means to be willing to suffer for the sake of showing God's radical love.

"You have heard that it was said, 'Eye for eye, and tooth for tooth.' But I tell you, 'Do not resist an evil person. If someone strikes you on the right cheek, turn to him the other also'" (Matt. 5:38–39).

LEADER'S NOTES

Leading a Bible discussion—especially for the first time—can make you feel both nervous and excited. If you are nervous, realize that you are in good company. Many biblical leaders, such as Moses, Joshua, and the apostle Paul, felt nervous and inadequate to lead others (see, for example, 1 Corinthians 2:3). Yet God's grace was sufficient for them, just as it will be for you.

Some excitement is also natural. Your leadership is a gift to the others in the group. Keep in mind, however, that other group members also share responsibility for the group. Your role is simply to stimulate discussion by asking questions and encouraging people to respond. The suggestions listed below can help you to be an effective leader.

PREPARING TO LEAD

1. Ask God to help you understand and apply the passage to your own life. Unless that happens, you will not be prepared to lead others.
2. Carefully work through each question in the study guide. Meditate and reflect on the passage as you formulate your answers.
3. Familiarize yourself with the leader's notes for each session. These will help you understand the purpose of the session and will provide valuable information about the questions in the session.
4. Pray for the various members of the group. Ask God to use these sessions to make you better disciples of Jesus Christ.
5. Before the first session, make sure each person has a study guide. Encourage them to prepare beforehand for each session.

LEADING THE SESSION

1. Begin the session on time. If people realize that the session begins on schedule, they will work harder to arrive on time.
2. At the beginning of your first time together, explain that these sessions are designed to be discussions, not lectures. Encourage everyone to participate, but realize some may be hesitant to speak during the first few sessions.
3. Don't be afraid of silence. People in the group may need time to think before responding.

4. Avoid answering your own questions. If necessary, rephrase a question until it is clearly understood. Even an eager group will quickly become passive and silent if they think the leader will do most of the talking.

5. Encourage more than one answer to each question. Ask, "What do the rest of you think?" or "Anyone else?" until several people have had a chance to respond.

6. Try to be affirming whenever possible. Let people know you appreciate their insights into the passage.

7. Never reject an answer. If it is clearly wrong, ask, "Which verse led you to that conclusion?" Or let the group handle the problem by asking them what they think about the question.

8. Avoid going off on tangents. If people wander off course, gently bring them back to the passage being considered.

9. Conclude your time together with conversational prayer. Ask God to help you apply those things that you learned in the session.

10. End on time. This will be easier if you control the pace of the discussion by not spending too much time on some questions or too little on others.

We encourage all small group leaders to use *Leading Life-Changing Small Groups* (Zondervan) by Bill Donahue while leading their group. Developed and used by Willow Creek Community Church, this guide is an excellent resource for training and equipping followers of Christ to effectively lead small groups. It includes valuable information on how to utilize fun and creative relationship-building exercises for your group; how to plan your meeting; how to share the leadership load by identifying, developing, and working with an "apprentice leader"; and how to find creative ways to do group prayer. In addition, the book includes material and tips on handling potential conflicts and difficult personalities, forming group covenants, inviting new members, improving listening skills, studying the Bible, and much more. Using *Leading Life-Changing Small Groups* will help you create a group that members love to be a part of.

Now let's discuss the different elements of this small group study guide and how to use them for the session portion of your group meeting.

THE BIG PICTURE

Each session will begin with a short story or overview of the session theme. This is called "The Big Picture" because it introduces the central theme of the session. You will need to read this section as a group or have group members read it on their own before discussion begins. Here are three ways you can approach this section of the small group session:

- As the group leader, read this section out loud for the whole group and then move into the questions in the next section, "A Wide Angle View." (You might read the first week, but then use the other two options below to encourage group involvement.)
- Ask a group member to volunteer to read this section for the group. This allows another group member to participate. It is best to ask someone in advance to give them time to read over the section before reading it to the group. It is also good to ask someone to volunteer, and not to assign this task. Some people do not feel comfortable reading in front of a group. After a group member has read this section out loud, move into the discussion questions.
- Allow time at the beginning of the group for each person to read this section silently. If you do this, be sure to allow enough time for everyone to finish reading so they can think about what they've read and be ready for meaningful discussion.

A WIDE ANGLE VIEW

This section includes one or more questions that move the group into a general discussion of the session topic. These questions are designed to help group members begin discussing the topic in an open and honest manner. Once the topic of the session has been established, move on to the Bible passage for the session.

A BIBLICAL PORTRAIT

This portion of the session includes a Scripture reading and one or more questions that help group members see how the theme of the session is rooted and based in biblical teaching. The Scripture reading can be handled just like "The Big Picture" section: You can read it for the group, have a group member read it, or allow time for silent reading. Make sure everyone has a Bible or that you have Bibles available for those who need them. Once you have read the passage, ask the question(s) in this section so that group members can dig into the truth of the Bible.

SHARPENING THE FOCUS

The majority of the discussion questions for the session are in this section. These questions are practical and help group members apply biblical teaching to their daily lives.

SNAPSHOTS

The "Snapshots" in each session help prepare group members for discussion. These anecdotes give additional insight to the topic being discussed. Each "Snapshot" should be read at a designated point in the session. This is clearly marked in the session as well as in the leader's notes. Again, follow the same format as you do with "The Big Picture" section and the "Biblical Portrait" section: Either you read the anecdote, have a group member volunteer to read, or provide time for silent reading. However you approach this section, you will find these anecdotes very helpful in triggering lively dialogue and moving discussion in a meaningful direction.

PUTTING YOURSELF IN THE PICTURE

Here's where you roll up your sleeves and put the truth into action. This portion is very practical and action-oriented. At the end of each session there will be suggestions for one or two ways group members can put what they've just learned into practice. Review the action goals at the end of each session and challenge group members to work on one or more of them in the coming week.

You will find follow-up questions for the "Putting Yourself in the Picture" section at the beginning of the next week's session. Starting with the second week, there will be time set aside at the beginning of the session to look back and talk about how you have tried to apply God's Word in your life since your last time together.

PRAYER

You will want to open and close your small group with a time of prayer. Occasionally, there will be specific direction within a session for how you can do this. Most of the time, however, you will need to decide the best place to stop and pray. You may want to pray or have a group member volunteer to begin the session with a prayer. Or you might want to read "The Big Picture" and discuss the "Wide Angle View" questions before opening in prayer. In some cases, it might be best to open in prayer after you have read the Bible passage. You need to decide where you feel an opening prayer best fits for your group.

When opening in prayer, think in terms of the session theme and pray for group members (including yourself) to be responsive to the truth of Scripture and the working of the Holy Spirit. If you have seekers in your group (people investigating Christianity but not yet believers) be sensitive to your expectations for group prayer. Seekers may not yet be ready to take part in group prayer.

Be sure to close your group with a time of prayer as well. One option is for you to pray for the entire group. Or you might allow time for group members to offer audible prayers that others can agree with in their hearts. Another approach would be to allow a time of silence for one-on-one prayers with God and then to close this time with a simple "Amen."

LOVING LESSONS
Hebrews 10:22–25

INTRODUCTION

As you begin this series of interactions, you will see very quickly that this is not a self-improvement course. This is not going to be a session where I offer a few helpful hints, sloganize and sentimentalize the whole concept of love. We're going to be talking about how it is that God moves people with His love so that they can love others with a supernatural love like His.

As you begin this series, it doesn't matter where each of your group members is with respect to their natural loving capacity. The good news all of us need to discover is that our God stands ready, willing, and able to explode the natural limits to our loving capacities. He can expand parameters with an enabling power and a supernatural capacity to love others that we didn't realize was even possible. It doesn't make any difference where we start or how bruised we are. God wants to move all of us from our natural ability to love into His supernatural kind of love.

THE BIG PICTURE

Take time to read this introduction with the group. There are suggestions for how this can be done in the beginning of this leader's section.

A BIBLICAL PORTRAIT

Read Hebrews 10:22–25

Question Two In the Old West, when a horse would not get moving, sometimes the rider would give a little kick with his spurs to get the animal's attention and to move it along. There was a need for some pointed motivation. This is the same with us today when it comes to the topic of love. Most of us need a little encouragement to keep growing in love. The writer of Hebrews calls us to be serious and intentional about motivating, pushing, "spurring on" other Christ followers to become more and more loving.

Allow time for group members to express how they can live out the encouragement of this passage.

SHARPENING THE FOCUS

Read Snapshot "You Matter to God" before Question 3

Question Three Some years ago I spent some time with a
national expert on the various cults that were popping up all
over the land. I asked him why so many people involve themselves with these groups. What do the cults really do for
people? The expert said that initially, most people are attracted
to the leaders of cults because they are looking for love. Most
of the people who hook up with those types of groups come
from loveless families. They have very few friends, if any.
They're drifting aimlessly. They're crying out for a little love
somewhere. Sadly, they're looking in all the wrong places.
The leaders of the cults and groups that attract these love-
seeking wanderers often use and abuse them, but rarely really
love them.

Christianity is completely different. Even the novice, the
seeker who takes the Bible in his hands for the first time and
flips through just a few pages, sees it in bold print. God puts
Himself on the line and expresses His love without reservation.
He shows His hand. He says, "I won't make any mystery
about it. I'm going to come right out and tell all of you in print
that you matter to Me. You can laugh at that claim; you can
reject it; you can do anything you want with it. But learn to
live with it, you matter to Me! I'm going to say it over and
over and over and over again. I love you." That's an amazing
statement for God to make.

Read Snapshot "Love in Action" before Question 4

Question Five I came from a religious home, where I grew
up with the impression that if you were ever going to make it
to heaven, you had to work and earn your way. At an early
age, I thought I was pretty smart and decided God would
never close the doors of heaven to a missionary. So I decided
that is what I would be. If that's what it took to gain assurance
of entrance into the kingdom of heaven, I'd be a missionary. I
also wanted to be a missionary in the furthest place possible.
Not Honolulu or some nice place like that. I wanted it to hurt.
I wanted guaranteed assurance!

I was appeasing God, working and striving and trying to merit
His acceptance and approval. And then, when I was sixteen
years old, a Bible verse struck me with a vengeance. In Titus
3:5 it says, "He saved us, not because of righteous things we
had done, but because of his mercy." Not by good works, but
because of His love. He did what had to be done. He paid the

price through the death of Jesus Christ to save us. I'll never forget the moment that it struck me as I walked from a meeting to my cabin at a Bible camp. I made a quick detour and went down and sat next to a leader on the lifeguard stand overlooking the lake. I must have said fifteen times, "I can't believe He loves me that much. I matter to Him." Then I wondered why noone had told me how much I mattered to Him. Everybody had been telling me to work and strive harder. Why hadn't anybody told me that I mattered enough for Him to save me instead of me trying to save myself?

That gripped me. I knew I had committed a lot of sins and had done a lot of things I regretted. But I'll tell you, the inside of my life has never been the same from that night on. That changed all my definitions of love. And I've been growing in my understanding of His love ever since.

The above story describes a starting point. If we are going to become loving people, there first must be a life-altering experience with the love of God. This is why the apostle John teaches in 1 John 4:19 that the only reason we will really want to love other people is because God first loved us with a love so pure that it explodes in our hearts. When we know God's love, we start to look at people—and life—differently. This session is about a radical transformation that happens in the core of your being when you stumble into the love of God.

Read Snapshot "The Presence of the Holy Spirit" before Question 6

Question Seven When I was growing up in Michigan we always had two or three airplanes associated with our family company. My dad used to send me out at the beginning of winter and say, "You need to put lightbulbs in the engine compartments of those airplanes because the hangers aren't heated, and the only way those motors will start in the cold is if you put lightbulbs in them." I remember the first time I went out there. I said, "What is this little lightbulb going to do when it's twenty below?" He said, "Just put that spotlight right in the engine compartment and see what happens." Sure enough, the next day when I went out after the lights had been on for twenty-four hours in twenty-degree-below zero weather, it started right up.

The Holy Spirit works much like that. When He dwells in our hearts the hardness begins to soften. A cold heart begins to warm. The presence of the Spirit is a radically transforming power in our lives. Sometimes the change happens quickly, sometimes more slowly. However, when the Spirit is in us, He will always make a difference.

Read Snapshot "A New Community" before Question 8

Question Nine Ask anyone who knows anything about our prison system in this country how to make someone a criminal, and they'll tell you to put them in prison for a long period of time and they'll come out a criminal. Hatred is contagious. But I believe the flip side is true also. Love is contagious too.

God wants all of us to catch the "love" disease. He not only puts the Holy Spirit inside of us, He places us in a church and surrounds us with people who are also diligently seeking to become better at loving. Hebrew 10:24 commands us to challenge each other to be more loving.

I'll never forget one of the times we had a food drive at our church. I felt so proud. I drove up in my Oldsmobile and took four bags of groceries out of the trunk. I thought I was doing something pretty great. As I was walking toward the church, I saw a beat up Dodge Dart. It looked like it had been through a war. But behind this car were about fifteen bags of groceries someone was giving to help others in need. I thought to myself, *Here is somebody who probably doesn't have half the means that I have, and yet they were moved to give far more than I did.* That challenged me. It didn't discourage me—it challenged me. I realized that is what the Bible means when it says to spur one another to love and good deeds.

PUTTING YOURSELF IN THE PICTURE

Let the group members know you will be providing time at the beginning of the next meeting for them to discuss how they have put their faith into action. Let them tell about how they have acted on one of the two options above. However, don't limit their interaction to these two options. They may have put themselves into the picture in some other way as a result of your session. Allow for honest and open communication.

Also, be clear that there will not be any kind of a "test" or forced reporting. All you are going to do is allow time for people to volunteer to talk about how they have applied what they learned in the previous session. Some group members will feel pressured if they think you are going to make everyone report on how they acted on these action goals. You don't want anyone to skip the next group because they are afraid of having to say they did not follow up on what they learned from the prior session. The key is to provide a place for honest communication without creating pressure and fear of being embarrassed.

Every session from this point on will open with a look back at the "Putting Yourself in the Picture" section of the previous session.

TENDER LOVE

Ephesians 4:29–32

INTRODUCTION

There is a multiplicity of reasons why some people are tender and others seem to be tougher. Part of it, I think, is the workmanship of God. He makes us all different. Part of it is family heritage, personality, temperament, reaction to life experiences, and so on. But thank God for tenderhearted people. I hate to think of what this world would be like without them. They stand in stark contract to those people who have a tougher temperament.

This session focuses specifically on those who would have to admit that they are a little on the tougher side of the continuum. I'm going to try and challenge you tougher hearts to see that there is some softening that has to happen in your life if you ever expect to grow in your capacity to love. I'm going to show you that you need to be kind, gentle, and tenderhearted toward others.

THE BIG PICTURE

Take time to read this introduction with the group. There are suggestions for how this can be done in the beginning of this leader's section.

A WIDE ANGLE VIEW

Question One You see it in airports or public places like shopping centers. An elderly woman who is struggling with luggage or packages and a steady stream of able-bodied people passing by her. Some will even sort of scowl and say, "Get a move on it, Grandma." And then a tenderhearted guy or gal will come along and take the time to give assistance. Tenderhearted people in this world react one way, and tough-hearted people seem to react in another way.

When Jesus told the parable of the Good Samaritan, He said that there were some religious people who still had a problem with tough-heartedness. The priest and the Levite had passed the beaten-up traveler on the other side of the road. They didn't want to get involved. Their hearts were hard even though they were religious leaders. Then came along a Samaritan, who gave assistance because he had a tender heart. We all have stories about those tenderhearted people who have impacted our lives.

There's a family in our church who some time ago had a dog that was a loyal, faithful part of their family for thirteen years. The health of the pet had deteriorated to a point that the only kind thing to do was have it put to sleep. However, they agonized over having to do that. They postponed it and postponed it until finally all of the members of the family except the dad were going to be out of town for some occasion or another. The dad decided this was the time to take the dog to the vet and have it put to sleep.

He said, "I picked the dog up and I carried it gently out to our car. As I drove to the veterinarian, the dog crawled up on the seat and came over and put its head right on my leg and nuzzled a little bit. I looked at our family pet of more than a decade and sadly knew this had to be done for his own good. I had such a hard time doing it though, it broke my heart. When I got to the vet, I picked up the dog and walked in. I explained the situation to the vet and the vet agreed to put the dog to sleep. Afterward, I went back out to the parking lot and sat for awhile and eventually went to work."

This man and his brother worked together. He said, "When I walked into the office my brother asked me where I had been. As I sat in his office and said, 'Well, today was the day that I had to take the dog over to the vet to be put to sleep.'" And the brother said, "You *paid* a vet to put the dog to sleep? You should have brought it over to me. I would have taken care of it. No problem." Here were two brothers from the same home, parents, family, and similar upbringing. One pretty tender, and the other a whole lot tougher in spirit.

A BIBLICAL PORTRAIT

Read Ephesians 4:29–32

Questions Two & Three The apostle Paul gives some great guidelines on how to avoid being tough-hearted and how to develop a tender heart. This passage calls us to speak words that build others up, to be kind, filled with compassion, and forgiving. It's a formula that will help even the toughest person move in the right direction. Also, there are some warnings and things we are called to purge out of our lives. If we are going to have tender hearts, we need to get rid of unwholesome talk, bitterness, rage, anger, a fighting spirit, slanderous words, and every form of malice. As we seek to develop the good and get rid of the bad, we will find our hearts growing more and more tender.

SHARPENING THE FOCUS

Read Snapshot "Tough-Hearted People" before Question 4

Question Four In the moments of quiet reflection which tough-hearted people experience, usually when we endure a financial setback, an accident, an illness, a divorce, or whatever it is that makes us think a little bit, we look into the mirror of our souls and often don't like what we see—especially those of us who have already come into a saving relationship with Jesus Christ.

On those occasions of introspection in my own life, I have wondered how my heart can still be so tough. I've experienced the personal love of Jesus Christ firsthand. Authentically, I feel His love for me. It has marked my soul and changed me. I know that the Holy Spirit resides in my life. I know He's working me over from the inside, trying to make me a more loving man. I know He has graciously put me in a community of brothers and sisters who are growing in their attempt to become more loving people. But I'm still too calloused and cold. What is still required from me to become a more tenderhearted person? What practical steps can I take to relate to people in a more tender fashion?

Have you ever asked those kinds of questions? Do you ever get sick and tired of your own tough-heartedness and all of the bruises and bumps and hurts you create as you move throughout life? Do you ever say you would love for somebody to show you how to become a little more tender? That is the central message of this session. If you stay tuned in, you will gain some practical skills for becoming a more tender person.

Read Snapshot "A New Look at People" before Question 5

Question Five Shortly after I became a Christian, I realized I had a whole lot of softening that needed to happen. Though I'm still a little tough, I'm a bowl of jello compared to what I use to be like more than two decades ago. I remember searching the Scriptures for practical suggestions. I needed help on how I could become kind and gentle—tenderhearted toward other people. Then I ran across an episode of the life of Jesus where He healed a blind man. Usually when Jesus healed blind people in the New Testament, He just touched them or spoke to them and their blindness was cured. They received their sight. This particular case is recorded in Mark 8. Jesus performed a two-phase healing. He touched the man's eyes first, and then He asked the man if he could see. The man said, "Well, I can see, but I see men walking around like trees. It's all blurry and fuzzy to me." And then Jesus touched him again and he received his whole sight and saw people clearly.

Some of us are in a lifelong process of seeing people more clearly. Although this passage is primarily about Jesus' compassion and power to heal, I feel there is another lesson as well. Some of us need the touch of Jesus over and over and over again as we learn to get a new look at people and see them clearly.

Read Snapshot "Slow Down" before Question 6

Questions Six & Seven If tough-hearted people could only realize how much every single person matters to God. If tough-hearted people could only understand that people are not just part of the landscape. If we could see that people are the most precious commodity on the planet in God's eyes. If tough-hearted people could understand that they've never bumped into just an ordinary person.

Every living, walking, breathing human being is an extraordinary treasure in the eyes of God. Every one of them. All people. The so-called lightweights, losers, and basket cases matter to God every bit as much as the heavyweights, winners, and survivors. A spiritually-confused Russian or Cuban or Palestinian matters as much to God as a spiritually-confused American. A fouled-up prisoner, homosexual, skid-row bum or bag lady matters every bit as much to God as a fouled-up stockbroker, dental student, CPA, or seminarian. They're all His creations. He's got a stamp on all of them. They're all the object of His affection. They're all invited to receive forgiveness at the cross. They're all invited into the family of God through Christ. And for those of us who already know Christ, every person we bump into out in the world is a potential brother or sister. They all matter to God—more than you and I will ever understand. If we could only grasp that truth. If we could only slow down enough to see people for who they really are and what they mean to God. Then we would soften up.

Next time you're rude to a waitress because she is only a waitress, stop. There is no such thing as "only a waitress." Next time you're rude to a parking lot attendant or a traffic

safety team member or the butcher or the baker or the candle-
stick maker—the next time you are rude to any of those people
because they're only a this or they're only a that—stop.
These people are extraordinary in the sight of God. They
matter to God.

Employers, next time you're going to give an employee a pink
slip—and you might have to do that—remember that that
employee matters to God. What about those of you who are
dating and you say you have to "dump" the person that you've
been dating? That's the way we talk isn't it? "Hey, I'm going
to dump her." "I'm going to dump him." Remember, you're
dumping a person who matters a lot to God. Now, maybe you
do need to break up. I'm not saying that all relationships are
permanent. But that person that you're breaking it off with
matters to God. Try to treat him tenderly. Treat all God's
treasures tenderly.

**Read Snapshot "Walking in Their Shoes" before
Question 8**

Question Eight Lynne and I try to have a date night every
week to keep our own relationship growing and vital. One
evening some years ago we wanted to see a movie, and were
choosing between a comedy and a heavier drama. Lynne kind
of wanted to see the drama, but I was a little nervous about it,
because I know that heavier dramas sometimes really affect
her. We finally did decide on a drama—a movie called
"Sophie's Choice."

I went and bought popcorn and sat down and put my arm
around her. I had a little twinkle in my eye . . . if you know
what I mean. Things were fine until about three-quarters of
the way through the show when it started to get a little bit
intense. It came to the point where Sophie has to decide, as
she is holding two children in her arms, which child she is
going to hand over to the Nazi officer for certain execution. It
came to that part of the movie and I thought, "Boy, this is
pretty heavy drama right here. It's getting a little long though.
I wonder if the popcorn stand is still open, because I would
like to get one more box before we go."

As I turned and looked, Lynne was sobbing and had almost
slid under the seats. So I brought her back up. She cried through
the rest of the movie. We walked out to the car and I could tell
that this was not a time for cracking jokes or anything. I was
this close to saying, "I told you we should have seen a comedy."
But even I'm not that insensitive. We cruised home quietly.
Didn't say a word. Went to bed. A day-and-a-half later, when

she could bring herself to it, she finally said, "I want to tell you why I was so upset." She said, "I just pictured having Todd in this arm and Shauna in this arm and having thirty seconds to make a choice which one was going to live and which one was going to die. And how in the world would I ever make that choice?" And I was thinking to myself, *She not only crawled into Sophie's shoes, but socks, dress, bonnet. You name it, she was Sophie.*

Tenderhearted people empathize so easily. They can crawl right into other people's skin. That makes it a little rough going to movies like the one above, but I'll tell you something: My wife has a very tender spirit toward other people in need. We enjoy giving a significant portion of our income away. And if Lynne had her way, we wouldn't have any spending money left. Because she just loves people. Every time she sees a need, she empathizes with it.

Tough-hearted people are going to have to work for the rest of their lives on developing empathy. It doesn't come as naturally to us. Tough-hearted people need to slow down and make a determined effort to put themselves in the shoes of other people for just a few minutes. It would soften us up. We need to hear some hard questions. What would it feel like to have a handicapped child? What would it feel like to be in a wheelchair? What would it feel like to be unemployed and have a mortgage, a car payment, and kids looking at you? What would it feel like to be black in a white society that isn't particularly sensitive to black people? What would it feel like to be hungry? What would it feel like to be divorced, to be a widow, to lose a spouse, to have cancer? If tough-hearted people would take the time to try and empathize, you would begin to see some cracks in the concrete that surrounds the hard hearts of tough people.

Read Snapshot "WWJD?" before Question 9

Question Nine Some of you are saying, "Well, what if I do that? What if I start seeing people for who they really are—treasures of God—and start empathizing with people and feeling these feelings of tenderness? How do I express that to people? I mean, what do you want me to do? Should I give away this store? Should I sell my house? What are you asking? What is God asking me to do?"

I think Scripture, in a nutshell, would say that if you want to know what the basic ground rules are, just treat people the way Jesus Christ treats you. The best definition of love that I've ever heard is, *treat other people in your life the way that Christ treats you.*

You say, "Well, how's that?" Well, whenever you pray, you have a promise don't you? That our Lord will listen attentively to every word you say. Why don't you treat your spouse that way? Why don't you treat your kids that way? Why don't you treat your coworkers that way? Slow down and turn off the television and close the door and say, "I'm going to listen, because I really want to hear what you have to say."

Another thing that the Lord does is that He *speaks truthfully to us.* Why don't you speak truthfully to some people? Why don't you deal fairly? Christ always deals fairly. He is a just God. He deals fairly with all of us. We should follow His example and show no partiality or discrimination.

Christ also *expresses His affection regularly.* If you are a believer, you can open the Bible and you see this on every other page. God says, "I'll take the risk. You are precious in My sight. I'll come right out and say it, 'I love you.'" If you walk with the Lord, the Holy Spirit will say to your spirit, "You are My son. You are My daughter. You are precious in My sight. I'm walking with you today. Trust in Me. I love you." God doesn't want any of His children walking around wondering whether or not they're loved. So why don't you treat people in your life just like Christ treats you? Why don't you express your affection regularly? Why don't you tell your wife or your husband regularly how much they mean to you? And why don't you say it to your kids regularly or to your folks, your coworkers, your neighbors? Why don't you express that regularly like Christ does to you? Just treat people the way that Christ treats you.

Christ *forgives us readily.* Before you leave this session it would be good to identify at least one person you need to forgive. It could be your spouse, kids, or a friend. Commit yourself to go to that person and say, "It's over. I want to be tender toward you. Christ treats me tenderly. He's forgiven me readily. Let's stop fighting. I forgive you."

Christ *gives bountifully.* Why don't we give bountifully? Why don't we get a little more outrageous with our grace toward each other? Christ encourages us continually. Why don't we do that? Why don't we just treat people that way? Whenever you're in doubt as to how to act toward other people if you are trying to act tenderly toward them, just treat people the way Christ treats you.

PUTTING YOURSELF IN THE PICTURE

Challenge group members to take time in the coming week to use part or all of this application section as an opportunity for continued growth.

TOUGH LOVE

Ephesians 4:14–16

INTRODUCTION

This session is meant to instruct and inspire the tenderhearted so that they can learn about a type of love that is often foreign to their experience. It's called tough love. This is valid, necessary, and biblical love. Speaking the truth even when the truth cuts and hurts. Making waves in relationships that shouldn't be stagnant. Doing some rebuking now and then. Correcting someone before they shipwreck their lives. My prayer is that God would use His spirit to challenge you to grow in your commitment to both tender and tough love.

THE BIG PICTURE

Take time to read this introduction with the group. There are suggestions for how this can be done in the beginning of this leader's section.

A WIDE ANGLE VIEW

Question One We find in Scripture that Jesus often demonstrated tough love. Tough love is quite often painful, but it is a very potent type of love. Here are some of the hard words that have been said to me over the years. "Billy, you don't get supper tonight. You head down to your room. Mistakes are one thing—lies are another." "The next time you talk to your mother like that will be on the way out the door when you are going apartment shopping." "Bill, why is it that you feel like you need to impress people?" Or "You know I love you, but I'm not going through with this wedding. You're not mature enough. I don't think I am either." Or "What's happened to you, Hybels? You're messed up. You used to have your head on straight, but I don't even know who you are anymore." Or "You might call this a marriage. I call it a joke. And I'm not going to let you continue to treat me like yesterday's mail." Or "Why is it that I feel like I can't disagree with you? Are you always right?" I could go on and on. I've had a lot of tough words said to me.

Why would anyone say such brutal things to me? First of all, most of those hard words said to me were absolutely true. Hard but true. There comes a time when the truth must be told, and it must be told straight. Simply because it's the truth. Sometimes we can't spare people from the truth. Sometimes we actually *harm* people when we don't tell them the truth.

Another reason why people have said those hard things to me over the years is because of the depth of their commitment to me. They simply love me too much to allow me to continue to act in a rebellious or deceitful or arrogant fashion. Some of these people said that God's reputation was at stake because I am a Christian. Other people have said that they just love me so much that they know I was going to ruin relationships if they didn't talk to me. Other people have spoken tough words because they didn't want Christ's ministry to be jeopardized by my behavior. Still others have spoken honestly because they don't want my marriage and family to be hurt. Many people over the years have taken off the gloves, rolled up their sleeves, and have taken me to the woodshed and made me face some things about myself. And I want to tell you, I love them for it. I really do.

A BIBLICAL PORTRAIT

Read Ephesians 4:14–16

Question Two This passage addresses three distinct elements of our faith and speaking the truth in love. First, it is a sign of maturity. Rather than being easily manipulated and swayed by false teaching and doctrines, we are able to articulate the truth of our faith. Our roots are deep, and we know where we stand.

Also, speaking the truth helps us grow in our relationship with Jesus because He is the "Truth." When we allow falsehood to mark and fill our relationships, it will eventually filter over into how we relate with Jesus. When we are truth-tellers who are willing to stand on the truth even when it hurts, we deepen our faith and our relationship with Jesus.

Strength in the body of Christ comes when we walk in the truth. This means we learn to express tough love as well as tender love. If we never speak the truth in love we will create a pseudo-community that is based on dishonesty. This is not reflective of the kingdom God is building. The church is strengthened when followers of Christ reflect His honest love, which includes both tenderness and toughness.

SHARPENING THE FOCUS

Read Snapshot "The Need for Balance" before Question 3

Question Three Tough love, admittedly, comes a bit easier for some. God sort of built some of us with tougher hearts. Some people can look at a situation when a relationship isn't progressing satisfactorily and can pinpoint the problem pretty easily. Some of us say, "What we need here is surgery. So what we're going to do is lay this guy out. We're going to get out a scalpel or a dull butter knife—doesn't matter much—and we're going to hack through some of the surface-level excuses and conversations and get right to the heart of the matter. If it causes a little bleeding, so be it. As long as the problem gets fixed, we're happy. We'll stitch the guy back up. Get him back on the road again. And if he survives the surgery, he'll thank us later." We're committed to fixing problems. We like to straighten things out, clear the air, get things off our chest. And you know what? There's a value to this. There are varying degrees of how tough this kind of love can be, but it can be very helpful and healing.

This is tough language for people with tender hearts. "Lay somebody out? Scalpel? Surgery? Blood? I don't have the stomach for that kind of thing. I never want to see that type of thing happen to anyone, let alone contemplate performing surgery myself some day." Tenderhearted people shrink back and say, "All I want is peace. All I want is tranquillity and harmony and handshakes and hugs and happiness. I want everyone to be nice to each other, and I want problems to solve themselves. And I want pain to go away." To the tender-hearted, God would say to you, "I understand your tender spirit. I made you that way. But if you're going to really learn how to love, you're going to have to learn about tough love."

One of my friends who is a staff member at Willow Creek Church is a true blue charter member of the tender hearts' club. He has a very soft temperament. In fact, he admits to the fact that he knew nothing about tough love until some of us brothers on staff had gotten around him and demonstrated tough love to him. He wrote a note to me before I preached on this topic, and said, "I'm praying for your tough love message. Tell those tenderhearted people that if brothers hadn't demon-strated tough love to me, I wouldn't have . . ." And then he made a little list for me. "I wouldn't have a growing relation-ship with my wife. I wouldn't have a ministry on the cutting edge of effectiveness. I wouldn't have a disciplined walk with Christ. I wouldn't have a righteous hatred of sin. I wouldn't have respect from the people I lead. I wouldn't have a Goliath-killing mentality. And I wouldn't have debts paid and money in the bank. But because of tough love, I have all of this stuff. So give those tenderhearted people a straight shot. Everybody needs some tough love lessons. I took his advice then, and I am taking it today. We can't compromise on tough love. If we do, it will hurt us, others, and the name of Jesus.

Read Snapshot "Truth-telling vs. Peacekeeping" before Question 4

Question Four Tenderhearted people not only appreciate peace and tranquillity in relationships, they kind of fixate on it. Tenderhearted people have a tendency to go to unbeliev-able lengths to avoid any kind of turmoil, unrest, or upheaval in a relationship. In fact, most tenderhearted people will go so far as to say, at least internally, "What I want in my relation-ship is peace at any price."

There's a little tension in a marriage, and the one partner says, "There's something wrong here. I can feel it. What's wrong?" And the answer comes back, "No, honey. Nothing is wrong. Really. Nothing at all." What the person is really saying is, "Well, something is wrong, but I don't want to be a pain. I don't want to create a hassle. I don't want to make a scene. I don't want any waves on our pond." And so they deliberately choose peacekeeping over truth-telling. They think it's a noble choice, but it's actually a bad choice. Because whatever caused that little tension is probably going to happen again and again. And it's going to get harder and harder to keep the peace. And then the poison is going to be manufactured and it's going to start to flow through your veins. And the spirit of disappointment will lead to a spirit of anger. And a spirit of anger to bitterness. And bitterness to hatred. And pretty soon, the relationship itself is dying. All the while, everything appears peaceful on the surface. Tenderhearted people say, "Peace at any price." Sadly, sometimes the price is the very relationship they are trying to save.

In the face of that kind of deception comes the bold counsel of the Lord written clearly in His Word in Ephesians 4. One phrase says we "must put off falsehood." Stop telling lies to each other. The second phrase says, "Speak truthfully to his neigh-bor." Start telling the truth to each other in a loving way. What does that mean? It means something that makes tenderhearted people tremble to their bones. It means, "Okay, all you tender-hearted people who sense problems in a relationship, and who know the truth needs to be told. You're going to have to do something very courageous. You're going to have to step up, trust God, and take a risk. You're going to have to make some waves and rock some canoes. You're going to have to upset some apple carts. You're going to have to do what it takes to get to the heart of the troublesome issue." Choose truth-telling over peacekeeping, and trust God for the outcome.

Read Snapshot "Whose Well-being?" before Question 5

Question Five When are people finally going to say, "I love you so much that I have got to tell you that you are working yourself to death, and I love you too much to watch you do that without my saying something?" Or "I love you so much that I have to tell you that you are ruining your body by the way you eat. By the fact that you never exercise. You smoke. You drink too much. You are ruining your body. And I'm not going to stay silent any longer about it." Or "You are piling up an enormous amount of debt, and I hate to see you get into that kind of bondage. I love you so much that I've got to say it." Or how about this from your pastor to you? "I love you people so much that I'm concerned about those of you who are gaining the whole world, but you're losing your soul."

The big question is, Whose well-being are you concerned about right now? So concerned that you know you need to go and risk rocking the boat. You need to go and express some concern for the well-being of another person. Do you really love this person as much as you say you do? Do you love them enough to risk the relationship in order to spare them from harm or danger? Then don't shrink back. Just go to them and say, "I know that you are not going to like what I'm going to say to you. But I'm telling you that I love you so much. I can't just sit idly by and watch you destroy yourself. I can't do it anymore. Please understand that I'm not trying to run your life. I'm only trying to express my love for you."

Question Six I went to a close brother one time because I saw his life taking a bad turn. I took him to a restaurant and said, "You know, I'm just concerned about the direction your life is taking. I'm not trying to run your life. I'm just concerned about the direction of it." I expressed my honest concern. I spoke the hard truth in a loving way. He did everything but leap over the table and punch my lights out. He was very angry at my expression of concern for him.

So what did I do? Being the man of valor and courage that I am, I looked at him right in the eye, and said, "Sorry. I will never bring this up to you again." In a short time he shipwrecked his life.

I see him occasionally and have said to him four or five times. "I've failed you. I should have been on you like a shirt. I should have taken you to lunch every day. I should have told you to leap over that table and deck me if it would have made you feel any better." Maybe God would have used me if I would have been a little more tenacious. That experience still haunts me today.

**Read Snapshot "Opening Pandora's Box"
before Question 7**

Question Seven Please understand that I am not encouraging you to go out and attack people. I am simply encouraging you to do what Scripture says. Go to a brother, a sister, a husband, a wife, a son, a daughter. Go to whomever you have to go to if there's counterfeit peace in the relationship, and acknowledge the good parts of the relationship and gently make a confession that you've been telling them lies. Tell them that from here on out, you would like the relationship to be built on truthfulness.

You say, "Well, what's going to happen?" I wish I could guarantee to you that the person would say, "Oh, thank you very much for bringing this to my attention. I've always wanted to hear this ugly thing about myself." You might get a slammed door. You might get a pink slip. You might be in big trouble. But the way I see it, you're in big trouble now if you think that you have a relationship that's built on the foundation of deception. You're already in trouble. So trust God. Go speak the truth in love. Take the risk. Make some waves. See what God does over the long haul.

PUTTING YOURSELF IN THE PICTURE

Challenge group members to take time in the coming week to use part or all of this application section as an opportunity for continued growth.

SACRIFICIAL LOVE
John 3:16–17; 1 John 4:9–12

INTRODUCTION

We're often told that marital love should be a nonstop, romantic epic. That love in friendships should be an uninterrupted series of beer commercials where old college buddies toast everyone's success and say "It doesn't get any better than this." Love is a flower. Love is a rose. Love is a many-splendored thing. But why doesn't love ever work out that way for most of us?

In this session we will take a whole new look at love. Rather than seeing it as a fluffy feeling of constant romance, excitement, or perfect harmony, we will learn that love involves deep sacrifice and commitment. This love lesson gets into the reality that love involves a deep giving of ourselves. Our ultimate example of sacrificial love is found in Jesus, who gave His own life for His friends. We are called to follow His example.

A WIDE ANGLE VIEW

Question One I don't know about you, but I have found that loving and caring and serving is a whole lot more closely related to work than to play. It has a whole lot more to do with servanthood than hero-hood. When I set about the task of loving, I usually end up giving instead of receiving. I still don't know anything about roses or many-splendored things. I don't experience the endless bliss of romance novels or the easy camaraderie of beer commercials.

It seems to me that whenever I try this thing called loving, I find that it inevitably costs me something. It seems like it costs me time, energy, and resources. Coincidentally, these are the three commodities that are precious to me. I don't easily part with my time, energy, or resources. Because I have these things in limited quantities, I tend to protect them.

Tell me love can be demonstrated to other people without it costing me time, energy, and money and I will gladly involve myself. Tell me which line to stand in, which project to sign up for, which person to commit myself to—I'm ready. I'll join. I'll start right now. But look me straight in the eye and tell me that love is synonymous with sacrifice, that loving someone is going to require that I part with what is so precious to me, and I become very reluctant to commit myself. I don't want to sign dotted lines. I hesitate to volunteer or get involved. And I think it is high time to be honest about the costs associated with loving people.

A BIBLICAL PORTRAIT

Read John 3:16–17 and 1 John 4:9–12

Question Two It's time to strip away all of the glitter and false glamour that the world puts on loving. The fact is, the world's view of love is a myth and fantasy. It's high time we tell the truth about loving. Love is more a sacrificial thing than a splendored thing. One only needs to look at the ultimate expression of love in the Bible to see that truth portrayed.

One Monday I went to teach a Bible study for a group of men. I thought I would take a little different approach so I said, "I'll speak to any Bible verse that any of you can pull out of your memory. Does anybody have a Bible verse that you've committed to memory?" There was a silence for a little while. Finally one man said, "Well, there's this remote one. I don't know if anybody else here knows it. It's "'For God so loved the world that he gave his one and only Son, that whoever believes in him shall not perish but have eternal life.' Something like that." And I said, "Well, it's a good verse. It's not that remote. It's one of the more prominent verses in Christendom. Be that as it may, I commend you for having it memorized." And so I began to make some comments on this famous verse of the Bible.

"For God so loved" means that God was so concerned about the well-being of people who are precious to Him. God gave up, He parted with, He expended, He sacrificed someone very precious to Him—His son Jesus—for the sake of those that He was concerned about. That most famous verse of the Bible capsulizes the biblical definition of the essence of love. It is being so concerned about the well-being of other people that you decide to willingly give up, part with, expend, sacrifice whatever is required to meet their needs or contribute to their life. Usually that means giving up, expending, parting with or sacrificing time, energy, and resources.

The Bible says if that's the price which needs to be paid, pay it. Because the Bible goes on to say it will be worth it. It really will. God will be so pleased that He will reward you for expending yourself for the sake of others. In fact, the Bible says that sacrifice is precisely what will bring about great meaning and fulfillment and satisfaction.

SHARPENING THE FOCUS

Read Snapshot "A Worldly Perspective" before Question 3

Question Three I walked into a classroom my junior year of college and heard a professor say to his sleepy-eyed students, "True personal fulfillment will never come through self-gratification." And while the other students yawned, I sat on the edge of my chair thinking, "That is the boldest, most radical, counter-cultural statement that I have ever heard. That flies in the face of everything that has been taught to me." True fulfillment will never come through self-gratification. I thought to myself that that little Frenchmen had just parted company with 99 percent of the human race. He would go on in class to say things like, "True, lasting, personal fulfillment comes when a person gives himself away to God and gives himself away to people." Do you want the route to personal fulfillment and satisfaction? Do you want your spirit to flourish and be full? Then expend your life. Give away your time and part with your energy and resources. "Love the Lord your God with all your heart and with all your soul and with all your mind" (Matt. 22:37). And then "Love your neighbor as yourself" (v. 39).

This teacher, Dr. Gilbert Bilezikian, who has since become my mentor and friend, use to end certain lectures early. Then he would say, "If you say you love God, you should be so concerned with God's purposes, God's glory, God's plans that you just offer yourself up. You should give yourself up and be willing to sacrifice all that you do and all that you have to Him in worship and thanksgiving." And then He would say, "What else does loving God mean? You say you love God. Talk is cheap. If you love somebody, you are concerned about their needs, their purposes, their plans, their glory, their well-being. So if you love God, be concerned about His glory. Be concerned about His plans. Be concerned about His purposes. And be willing to lay down your life as worship."

Remember Jesus' statement, "Do you really want to find life? Then lose your life." Give life to others, and you'll find life. Do you want to be a winner? Then get everyone else to stand in line in front of you. Do you want to be first? Then you be last and push others up first, and you'll end up feeling first. Do you want to be great in God's eyes? Be the servant of all.

The world writes books entitled, "Think and Grow Rich." Jesus would write books saying, "Love and Expend Yourself." Serve. Part with that which is precious to you. If you do, the end product will be a type of fulfillment and satisfaction the world will never experience.

Read Snapshot "True Gratification" before Question 4

Question Four There is tremendous power in examples. Allow time for group members to tell their stories of the heroes of faith they have known who have sacrificially given themselves in love to others.

Read Snapshot "Sacrificial Love in Marriage" before Question 5

Question Five The wisdom of the world says to guard your time and conserve your energy. Protect your personal resources. The wisdom of the world says to make sure that if any partner in the marriage is going to get the upper hand, it's going to be you. Too often the underlying objective in modern-day marriages is maximum personal pleasure with minimum personal sacrifice.

The wisdom of the Word of God is completely different. God says that each partner should look their spouse straight in the eye and say, "I love you." Which, by biblical definition means, "I am so concerned about your well-being that I am committing myself to serve you, to build you up, to cheer you on, knowing full well that it's going to cost me some time and a lot of energy and a lot of resources. But I want to put your interests in front of mine. I'll stand at the back of the line. You stand at the front. You go first. I'll serve you." And the other partner says, "No. You're saying what I want to say to you. I want you to go first. I want to go to the back of the line. I'm concerned about your well-being. I want to serve you, build you up, cheer you on." And instead of having a power struggle, each trying to gain the upper hand, there's a serving contest. Each partner in the marriage is trying to out-love and out-bless and out-serve the other. That is exactly the kind of marriage God wants for His followers. That's exactly the kind of sacrificial love that you can start demonstrating to your spouse if you follow the example of Jesus.

Read Snapshot "Sacrificial Love in Friendships" before Question 6

Question Seven I got a letter from a close Christian brother some time ago. We've been through a lot together. He wrote me a little note that said, "This letter is in part to tell you formally that whatever I have is yours. If you and your family ever need any kind of help, just say the word."

I was sitting around a campfire one time with one of our staff members who said, "One of the greatest blessings of my life is that I know right now that I could go to the phone and call five people. They would be there to help me. They would come to my side and help me with whatever resources they have." Those kinds of friendships don't grow on trees. The world doesn't know anything about them, but God is blessed by them. That's what life is about.

Putting Yourself in the Picture

Challenge group members to take time in the coming week to use part or all of this application section as an opportunity for continued growth.

STEADFAST LOVE
1 Samuel 30:6

INTRODUCTION

We are called to be loving. God gave us the greatest example of love by sending His own Son to this earth to be a perfect sacrifice of love for us. Our love should be tender and kind. It should also be tough. We need to learn to strike a balance between these two essential expressions of love. Our love is to reflect the sacrificial nature of Jesus' love. He gave himself completely for us, and we are to give ourselves sacrificially to each other. As we continue with our loving lessons, we will discover that this kind of love is impossible to maintain on our own.

Our own spiritual, emotional, and physical reserves are not enough to keep us going. We need to regularly refuel in each of these areas if we are going to love over the long haul. This session is about how we can keep our tanks full and our lives filled with love for God and others.

THE BIG PICTURE

Take time to read this introduction with the group. There are suggestions for how this can be done in the beginning of this leader's section of your small group study guide.

A BIBLICAL PORTRAIT

Read 1 Samuel 30:6

Question Two There is an amazing little phrase in 1 Samuel 30, verse 6, that has caught my attention for many years. I've wondered about it, thought about it, and meditated on it. It's the little phrase, "But David found strength in the LORD his God."

David, a man of unbelievable character and compassion, finds himself caving in, getting low on love, his tanks almost depleted. He is fighting off the temptation to abandon his leadership position. He is sick of the people. He's exhausted. He feels like quitting, but he also wonders if there is another way. Suddenly he realizes where he must go if he ever expects to be refueled for continued leading and loving. David suddenly remembers that he was never called to handle these loving challenges alone. I think David stopped and reassessed his situation, and to his own embarrassment, had to admit to God and himself that he had gotten so caught up in loving people, serving, leading, and assisting people that he had unwittingly neglected to keep his own spiritual fuel tanks filled. As many of us have learned over the years, it's impossible to love people over the long haul without keeping your own relationship with God fresh and growing and vital.

SHARPENING THE FOCUS

Read Snapshot "A Triangle of Steadfastness" before Question 4

Question Four One Sunday morning, after preaching about sacrificial and steadfast love, a young man came up to me and asked, "When are you going to get to the *real deep mysteries* and the real challenges of loving?" I looked at him and I said, "That's as deep as I go." If you don't think that we're talking about major league challenges, I don't know what you're looking for. This kind of love is very challenging to me.

If you are committed to growing in your capacity to love other people, if you are committed to improving your relationships, if you are committed to loving people who are difficult to love, you will quickly find that kind of love is extremely exhausting. You're going to be out there giving and serving and loving and expending and then you're going to come to a point where you feel sort of numbed out. You may even end up running on empty.

Read Snapshot "Empty and Angry" before Question 5

Question Five If you are a person who has been on the front lines of loving, you have reached the point along the way where you have thought to yourself, *I can't handle another person. I can't handle another heartache. I can't handle another need, another hurt. I want to run away, build a wall around myself, become a hermit.* The idea of living in a cabin somewhere deep in the woods starts to sound pretty good to you. Do you ever feel that way? Exhausted by the endless demands of loving people?

Every Christian solider who has ever fought on the front lines of loving people has come to that point. And if you haven't yet, you probably will. I actually hope you do. Because you will learn one of the most important lessons in all of life when you come to that point. When you come to the end of your own ability or capacity to love, you have reached a very important crossroad. You're going to have to learn how to refuel your tanks. You're going to have to learn how to replenish yourself so that you can go back to the front lines of loving people where God wants you to be.

When you come to that crossroad and you're all out of love, there is a great temptation to give up on loving people. I hear it all the time. People say, "I'm burned out on involvement with people. I use to be active. I use to be involved. I use to have relationships. I use to be in ministries around the church. But I got all burned out, and now I don't do any of that stuff. I've quit. I don't expend my time and my energies like I use to." These people are not just empty, they are angry.

We're not called to run the hundred-yard dash in loving people. We're called to run the marathon. And in order to do that, you've got to learn how to refuel yourself when you run out of love.

Read Snapshot "Refueling Your Spiritual Tank" before Question 6

Question Six Somehow we must learn how to slow our lives down, get off the treadmill, seek out solitude, and learn how to encourage ourselves in God. We have to learn how to replenish our own spiritual reserves. There are many practical ways to do that. Let me just give you a few to think about.

I suggest a daily time where you take a time-out—hopefully before your day even gets started. Sit down and find a place of solitude and say, "Lord, I know that I'm not going to be able to handle the demands and the rigors of loving today. And so I want to pray to You now, and I want to worship You now. I want to talk with You, and I want to read Your Word. I want to have the type of conversation that allows for You to regenerate my spiritual energies." Journaling and praying and worshipping God is a way you can be replenished every single day.

Another way is to listen to Christian music. So many times when I have to leave to go out on an appointment and all the demands, phone calls, and responsibilities are mounting, I put in a worship tape and allow the Spirit of God to replenish my spirit. Sometimes that half hour on the road listening to Christian music becomes a source of refreshment and strength. It's like Psalm 23, which reminds me that God knows how to restore my soul. Christian music tapes or message tapes are a way that you can refuel yourself.

I know of a man in my church who takes fifteen minutes reading the promises in the Word of God over his lunch hour almost every day. It replenishes him. I know people who take walks every night, during which they worship and relate to God. They get replenished in their spirit on those walks. I know people who play musical instruments to the Lord. I know people who read Christian books or who sing choruses to the Lord. The list is endless, but experiment until you find ways to refuel yourself spiritually. Because when you learn how to do that, you will have learned how to love sacrificially and steadfastly. And that is such a valuable lesson to learn.

I might also add that church-wide refueling opportunities are available and effective too. This can be on a Sunday or mid-week. It can be in a worship service or a small group. It's absolutely amazing what God will do when you avail yourself of a refueling opportunity, be it private or corporate. But if you think you can stay on the front lines of loving without learning how to refuel yourself spiritually, you're kidding yourself. You're going to let your tanks run dry. Watch your spiritual fuel gauge. You can't love with an empty tank. Find whatever practical ways you need to replenish yourself.

Read Snapshot "Refueling Your Emotional Tank" before Question 7

Question Seven Most of us have seen the charts put together by psychologists that illustrate the emotional toll taken when certain major life changes occur. Here are just a few off one of the standard charts.

The death of a spouse takes an enormous emotional toll on you. It's at the top of the list. If you've gone through a divorce, a marital separation, death of a family member, personal injury or illness. If you've been let go at work. If you've become pregnant. If there has been a business readjustment. A change in your financial state. A change in your residence. All of these have a tremendous impact on our emotional fuel reserves.

The point the experts are making is that just experiencing some of the ongoing, inevitable traumas of life will drain you emotionally. You can be doing great spiritually, but if you're drained emotionally, you're going to feel like you are all out of love and don't have anything to give other people. You're going to feel a certain type of detachment and disinterest in the well-being of others.

The experts tell us that there are really two primary ways to refuel our emotional tanks. The first is relaxation. Now, some

Type A personalities are already saying, "No. I want to replenish myself emotionally really fast. I want a pill. I want an injection. I don't want to just relax, because I like the fast track." That fast track is what keeps you emotionally depleted. The experts say that if you're ever going to replenish yourself emotionally, you need an old-fashioned, feet up, winding down, deep breaths, no phone calls break. Relaxation so that nature can take its course. And your emotional reserves can be replenished.

The other way to replenish yourself emotionally is recreation. Look at the word itself: Re-creating. These are certain activities that you find inspire you. They recreate a sense of enthusiasm for life. You can be emotionally depleted and go out and do your favorite form of recreation and come back two hours later and say, "I feel better now. I feel emotionally replenished."

I was challenging Lynne once during a time when her emotional reserves were low. As we were talking about that, she said, "You know what I think my problem is? I haven't been reading, writing, or playing my flute enough." She continued, "Each of those activities rejuvenates me. They inspire me." To be honest, trying to play the flute would not be a refueling experience for me. However, for many years I have found refreshment in sailing. Sailing is like therapy for me.

Every person is different, but I think that each person has some type of recreation that replenishes them emotionally. You've got to experiment and try different things. Do whatever it takes to come up with those things that really replenish you.

Read Snapshot "Keeping Your Physical Tank Full" before Question 8

Question Eight It's difficult to live with people who are run down physically, isn't it? This is, I suppose, a large part of why the Bible commands us to take care of our bodies. In 1 Corinthians 3 and 1 Corinthians 6, Paul says our bodies are a temple of the Holy Spirit. And not only that, but if you are ever going to have the energy to relate to people optimally, you're going to have to keep physically replenished.

How do you stay physically fit? Well, you know the three rules: eat right, sleep right, and exercise. All of these things work together to produce a type of physical vitality that will assist you in your attempts at loving people.

You need to eat right, which means not only the right quantities, but the right quality of food. You need to learn to stay away from sugar highs and sugar lows and fatty foods and all of those things that can destroy your physical vitality. Experts tell us it's medically proven that exercise replenishes energy levels, it doesn't deplete them. Wasn't it Jackie Gleason who said, "Whenever I feel the urge to exercise, I lay down until it goes away"? He was thinking that exercise will deplete his energy. But that's not true. So how are your physical reserves? What about your body? What about your eating and sleeping and exercise?

PUTTING YOURSELF IN THE PICTURE

Challenge group members to take time in the coming week to use part or all of this application section as an opportunity for continued growth.

RADICAL LOVE
Matthew 5:38–42

INTRODUCTION

Some situations require a love that goes even beyond the standard sacrificial and steadfast love we have been studying over the past weeks. Some people need a radical love that breaks through hard hearts. Some people are so tied up in their own anger and hostility that our usual efforts of love don't seem to make an impact. This is when Jesus calls us to extend a radical love that goes above and beyond what anyone would ever expect.

When we begin to love like Jesus, we will discover we have a capacity for radical acts of love that will even surprise us at times. Jesus loved radically, and He calls us to follow in His footsteps.

THE BIG PICTURE

Take time to read this introduction with the group. There are suggestions for how this can be done in the beginning of this leader's section.

A BIBLICAL PORTRAIT

Read Matthew 5:38–42

Question Two The highest priority in the life of every person should be to love God with all our heart, soul, mind, and strength. To worship Him. To give Him our lives. But Jesus said the second highest priority in all of life is to love people who matter to God in a radical, nonretaliatory, second-mile way.

There are some general applications for you regarding this that are as plain as can be. There's no mystery about them. For one, resentment and retaliation are dead-end roads. Revenge only perpetuates and escalates interpersonal animosity. Somebody has to stop the senseless escalation. That someone will most often be a fully devoted follower of Christ who is willing to express radical love. God would have it be you, and He would have it be me.

Another thing is that I must be less concerned about defending my male honor. I have to learn how to absorb some everyday slaps. Absorb the indignity of being cut off in traffic or someone cutting into line in front of me or butting into a conversation that I'm having. I need to become less defensive and learn how to absorb some shots instead of returning them.

And I also have to rediscover how much of an impact it makes on people when we surprise them with service above and beyond the call of duty, when we exceed the barest minimum of service. And, of course, I must continue to reevaluate how I avail my resources to those who need them. That means my money and my time and my energies.

Question Three For a couple thousand years people have read and prayed and asked the Spirit of God to help them understand and apply these four illustrations. Many believers have drawn a wide range of conclusions from these words spoken from the lips of Jesus. I think it's safe to say that this little section of the Sermon on the Mount will be a mirror for the souls of Christians until the end of history. At this point in my own spiritual development, I still shake my head and claim confusion over exactly how to apply some of these challenges. I still have many questions about the implications of these little stories.

However, we do need to avoid two extreme responses. This passage is not a call to mindless acceptance of all violence. We are called to be wise in our decisions and the way we love. It isn't a call to be poor stewards and to give away everything we have to the first person who puts out their hand. The other extreme is also dangerous ground. We can't rationalize these words away as only a call to be "kind and nice" to others. This is a radical call to sacrificial living and giving of ourselves beyond human expectations. When we accept the call to go above and beyond the call of duty, people see a love that marks them, breaks through resistances, and changes lives.

SHARPENING THE FOCUS

Read Snapshot "Outrageous Giving" before Question 4

Question Four The second illustration that Jesus mentioned requires a brief explanation about Middle Eastern wardrobes. The common-day wardrobe consisted of two parts. The first part was an inner garment of soft fabric worn close to the skin. Most people would have several sets of these inner garments. And then there was an outer garment, a heavy, very warm, loose-fitting garment that served a dual purpose. It was like a sports jacket or a suit coat during the day. At night, however, it served as a blanket. In that climate, a man without his outer garment for warmth at night was in a bad way. This outer garment was so important that it was protected by law. Nobody could keep another man's outer garment overnight as collateral.

It was common during trading and bartering sessions during the day for a deal to be made concerning the trading of food or wood or seed. The men would hold each other's cloaks or outer garments as collateral until the deal was consummated. But the Jewish law was clear. Even if a man didn't come through with his part of the deal, you still had to give him his cloak back at sunset or he might freeze to death.

Read Snapshot "Going the Extra Mile" before Question 5

Question Six The third illustration Jesus used cut to the very soul of His Jewish listeners because it had to do with a practice that was absolutely detested by all Jews. This was a practice called "impressment." Now we don't know much about that in this culture, but impressment was common practice in the days of Jesus. Israel, during those days, was part of the Roman Empire. Roman soldiers occupying Judean provinces could legally approach any Jew at anytime of the day or night and impress them or coerce them into service. They could force them to make their meals, and do their laundry and other menial tasks. That really angered the Jews. But something the Jews hated even more was when a Roman solider would make them carry his baggage. When there was a shift in the troop assignments, the Roman soldiers would come up and tap a Jewish citizen on the shoulder with a spear and say, " Here's my suitcase. There's a duffel bag. Carry it." They could be impressed into service in the middle of the night, while they were plowing a field, while they were selling their wares. In light of this, Jesus' words are even more radical. He was calling them to do something they absolutely despised, and He was calling them to do it willingly, beyond the expected norm of the day.

Read Snapshot "Why Such Radical Love?" before Question 7

Question Seven God knows it will take a radical love to break the cycle of interpersonal hostility that's existed ever since the book of Genesis, where we read that Cain killed his brother Abel. A friend who is a paramedic in a tough part of Chicago once said to me, "You know how it goes. It starts with a little misunderstanding. It escalates when someone's feelings get hurt, and that person uses a little sarcastic language. The sarcasm solicits a smart-mouth response, which brings a threat and then a challenge, which gets the male bravado and honor going. Then comes the fists and the clubs and the knives and the guns. Then the blood flows and the flesh tears. And when it's all over and people are laying in piles, they call us and we come in and pick up the pieces."

I know how it goes. It's been going that way for thousands of years. The endless, senseless cycle of interpersonal hostility. Now, most of our hostilities don't end in hand-to-hand combat. Most of our hostilities end in cold wars. Detachment, distrust, alienation, bitterness, a little name calling and mud slinging and separation and isolation and then lawsuits. We don't usually fight with our fists.

But do you see how the cycle of hostility must be stopped if there is ever to be any hope for relational harmony in this world? Why does Jesus insist that you and I become examples of radical, nonretaliatory, second-mile love? Because it will take people like us to break those senseless cycles. Somebody has to absorb a blow or an insult or a slap instead of returning one. Somebody has to absorb an injustice instead of inflicting another one on someone else. Someone has to diffuse the senseless escalation. Pull the plug of continued cruelty. Break the cycle of hostility. And God says let it be you and me.

Only radical lovers can break the cycle of interpersonal hostil-ities. Are you willing to be the first one in your marriage to break the icy silence when feelings have been hurt? Are you willing to be the family member who says, "Let's stop this nonsense. Let's stop it. I was wrong." Or how about in the workplace? Are you willing to be the one who says, "Let's sit down and work it out. I apologize. I'm sorry. Let's get on with it." Only radical love can break the cycle of interpersonal hostility. God says, "I'm looking for some followers who will love radically. Who will report for duty?"

Question Eight Another reason God challenges all of us to demonstrate radical, nonretaliatory, second-mile love is because nothing leaves a deeper mark on the lives of spiritual-ly-hardened men and women than radical love. If you already know the love of Jesus Christ in a personal way, you know He's wonderful. You know there are moments where you feel His love, His presence, and His power. And you wouldn't trade that for anything in the world. You're thrilled when you are used by Him, and you anticipate spending eternity with Him.

There is such a compelling power in the demonstration of radical love that calloused people's heads spin. They cannot figure you out when you demonstrate that kind of love. When they see a marriage or a family built on radical love, or a set of business relationships that operate with that kind of integrity, there is such convicting power in that. You take a slap. You refuse to return an insult. You serve someone with a second-mile attitude. You give up your rights now and then. You make your resources available in a generous fashion. You'll have people shaking their heads saying, "I just don't believe this. What is going on? This is so countercultural. Something other-worldly is going on here."

Jesus did that all of His life. He took slaps without saying anything. He absorbed beatings without cursing anyone back. When they pounded nails into His hands and feet, He turned to the people doing the pounding and said, "Father, these men matter to You. I would appreciate it if you wouldn't charge this crime to their account. Because they matter to You. They matter to Me. I would like them to be forgiven." He took ridicule on the cross. And before He died, He cried, "It is finished! I have paid the price of sin for all these precious people who have been scorning Me and mocking Me and ridiculing Me and beating Me. I have paid the price for all of these people who matter so much to You, Father."

At these words, a hardened Roman soldier broke down and cried, "Surely, this was the Son of God." I doubt he had ever read a theology book, but he was broken by the power of radical, nonretaliatory, second-mile love.

Your radical love can and will do something over time. It's the most powerful weapon you have. Why don't you use it? In the power of the Holy Spirit, why don't you use it? In your marriage, in your family, on the job site, in the school, at the clubs. Use it. If you do, God will use you to mark the lives of men and women with the power of radical love.

Question Nine I had lunch some years ago with a friend who was a pastor in a far away country. This man's father had started this particular ministry, and his son had continued it. A religious sect arranged for the execution of this man's father. They deceitfully asked his father if they could come in and have a time of private prayer with him. The father, of course, agreed. When they came, a man took a knife out of his cloak and stabbed my friend's father repeatedly. My friend came running into the room and picked up his father and watched him bleed to death in his arms. After this experience, this man asked me if I would come to his country to preach to the very sect of people who arranged for the execution of his father. I saw in the heart and the life of that man an unusual intimacy and connectedness with God—and a radical love.

When you are taking slaps, carrying other people's baggage and going the second mile, you tend to draw very close to the heart of God. The truth is, you have nowhere else to go. When you are out on the edge following Christ, you tend to cling to Him and to pray and to feel His presence in unusually powerful ways.

Some Christians don't want to leave the harbors of love. They've never gone out on the high seas of radical, nonretaliatory, second-mile love. But that's where the action is. That's where the adventure is. That's where the thrills are. That's where the presence of God manifests itself in a greater way than you can ever imagine.

PUTTING YOURSELF IN THE PICTURE

Challenge group members to take time in the coming week to use part or all of this application section as an opportunity for continued growth.

ADDITIONAL WILLOW CREEK RESOURCES

Small Group Resources

Leading Life-Changing Small Groups, by Bill Donahue

The Walking with God Series, by Don Cousins and Judson Poling

Evangelism Resources

Becoming a Contagious Christian (book), by Bill Hybels and Mark Mittelberg

Becoming a Contagious Christian (training course), by Mark Mittelberg, Lee Strobel, and Bill Hybels

Inside the Mind of Unchurched Harry and Mary, by Lee Strobel

Inside the Soul of a New Generation, by Tim Celek and Dieter Zander, with Patrick Kampert

The Journey: A Bible for Seeking God and Understanding Life

What Jesus Would Say, by Lee Strobel

Spiritual Gifts and Ministry

Network (training course), by Bruce Bugbee, Don Cousins, and Bill Hybels

What You Do Best, by Bruce Bugbee

Marriage & Parenting

Fit to Be Tied, by Bill and Lynne Hybels

Authenticity

Honest to God¿, by Bill Hybels

Descending into Greatness, by Bill Hybels

Ministry Resources

Rediscovering Church, by Bill Hybels

The Source, compiled by Scott Dyer, introduction by Nancy Beach

Christianity 101, by Gilbert Bilezikian

All of these resources are published in association with Zondervan Publishing House.

More life-changing small group discussion guides from Willow Creek

Walking with God Series
Don Cousins and Judson Poling

This series of six guides (and two leader's guides) provides a solid, biblical program of study for all of the small groups in your church. The Walking with God Series is designed to help lead new and young believers into a deeper personal intimacy with God, while at the same time building a strong foundation in the faith for all believers, regardless of their level of maturity. These guides are also appropriate for individual study. Titles in the series are:

Friendship with God: Developing Intimacy with God: 0-310-59143-0
The Incomparable Jesus: Experiencing the Power of Christ: 0-310-59153-8
"Follow Me!": Walking with Jesus in Everyday Life: 0-310-59163-5
Leader's Guide 1 (covers these first three books): 0-310-59203-8
Discovering Your Church: Becoming Part of God's New Community: 0-310-59173-2
Building Your Church: Using Your Gifts, Time, and Resources: 0-310-59183-X
Impacting Your World: Becoming a Person of Influence: 0-310-59193-7
Leader's Guide 2 (covers these last three books): 0-310-59213-5

Also available: *Walking with God Journal:* 0-310-91642-9

Look for the Walking with God *Series*
at your local Christian bookstore.

ZondervanPublishingHouse
Grand Rapids, Michigan

A Division of HarperCollinsPublishers

Helping People Become
Fully Devoted to Christ

This resource was created to serve you.

It is just one of many ministry tools that are part of the Willow Creek Resources® line, published by the Willow Creek Association together with Zondervan Publishing House. The Willow Creek Association was created in 1992 to serve a rapidly growing number of churches from all across the denominational spectrum that are committed to helping unchurched people become devoted followers of Christ.

The vision of the Willow Creek Association is to help churches better relate God's solutions to the needs of seekers and believers. Here are some of the ways it does that:

- **Church Leadership Conferences**—3½-day events, generally held at Willow Creek Community Church in South Barrington, IL, that are being used by God to help church leaders find new and innovative ways to fulfill and expand their ministries.
- **The Leadership Summit**—a once-a-year event designed to increase the leadership effectiveness of pastors, ministry staff, and volunteer church leaders.
- **Willow Creek Resources®**—to provide churches with a trusted channel of ministry resources in areas of leadership, evangelism, spiritual gifts, small groups, drama, contemporary music, and more. For more information, call Willow Creek Resources® at 800/876-7335. Outside the U.S. call 610/532-1249.
- **WCA Monthly Newsletter**—to inform you of the latest trends, events, news, and resources.
- **The Exchange**—to assist churches in recruiting key staff for ministry positions.
- **The Church Associates Directory**—to keep you in touch with over 1000 other WCA member churches.

For conference and membership information please write or call:

Willow Creek Association
P.O. Box 3188
Barrington, IL 60011-3188
(847) 765-0070